Under a Strong Wind

THE ADVENTURES OF
JESSIE BENTON FRÉMONT

An engraved portrait of Jessie Benton Frémont taken from a painting by Fagnini. (From Frémont and '49, *by Frederick S. Dellenbaugh, 1914.)*

*U*nder a Strong Wind

The Adventures of

Jessie Benton Frémont

by DOROTHY NAFUS

MORRISON

Illustrated with photographs and old prints

ATHENEUM · New York · 1983

LIBRARY OF CONGRESS CATALOGING IN PUBLICATION DATA

Morrison, Dorothy N.
Under a strong wind.

Bibliography: p. 169
Includes index.
SUMMARY: A biography of the woman who along with
her husband, an Army officer, explorer, and
legislator, took part in some of the most important
events of nineteenth-century America including the
exploration of the west and the formation of the
Republican party.
1. Frémont, Jessie Benton, 1824–1902—Juvenile
literature. 2. Frémont, John Charles, 1813–1890—
Juvenile literature. 3. Wives—United States—
Biography. [1. Frémont, Jessie Benton, 1824–1902.
2. United States—History—1849–1877—Biography.
3. United States—History—1865–1898—Biography]
I. Title.
E415.9.F79M67 1983   973.6'092'4 [B] [92] 83-6356
ISBN 0-689-31004-8

Text copyright © 1983 by Dorothy N. Morrison
Published simultaneously in Canada by
McClelland & Stewart, Ltd.
Composition by Service Typesetters, Austin, Texas
Printed and bound by
Fairfield Graphics, Fairfield, Pennsylvania
Designed by Mary Ahern
First Edition

For BOB
With love and thanks

AUTHOR'S NOTE

FEW WOMEN or men have had lives as exciting as that of Jessie Benton Frémont, whose story is the story of the nation. The South—the frontier—new, raw California—the Gold Rush—the infant Republican Party—the Civil War—she was part of them all.

People didn't agree about her husband, John Charles Frémont, during his lifetime, and even today some writers call him a hero, while others see him as a reckless blunderer. The truth lies somewhere between. Certainly he gave Americans information they needed, and he inspired his followers with his own derring-do. Just as certainly, by his own bad judgment or stiff-necked pride, he lost a huge fortune and twice wrecked his army career. However, since this is Jessie's book and she adored her Mr. Frémont, I have pictured him through her eyes, letting his actions speak for themselves.

Much of the information in this book comes from manuscripts and Jessie's own published writings. Wherever I use quotation marks, the enclosed words are taken exactly from some such primary source. As with my other biographies, I have not made up anything—conversations, characters or incidents.

Many people have helped me track down materials. I would like especially to thank the staff of the Bancroft Library of the University of California for helping me find my way through that vast collection; of the Beaverton City Library of Beaverton, Oregon, for patiently ordering book after book from the Interlibrary Loan Service; of the Multnomah County Library of Portland, Oregon, for letting me go to their warehouse to delve into stored volumes of ancient periodicals, and for their assistance in securing pictures.

Librarians are wonderful. I salute them all.

CONTENTS

Under a Strong Wind

THE ADVENTURES OF
JESSIE BENTON FRÉMONT

O N E

*O*ld South–New West

1824-1838

JESSIE BENTON clutched her injured arm as she darted down the shady lane toward the Big House. Just ahead ran a tall young slave named Wesley, with little Mac lying limp over his shoulder and blood streaming from the cut on Mac's forehead. The other Benton children—big sister Eliza, who was twelve, Sarah, age eight, and Randolph, age five—thudded along behind. But Jessie was thinking only of Mac, who was just four years old, and sick besides, with a racking cough. It was awful, having Mac hurt.

Cherry Grove, the Virginia plantation where Jessie and her family were visiting, stretched around them, warm in the sun, for thousands of acres to the peaks of the Blue Ridge Mountains. Today the children had walked a mile down the lane from the Big House to the workers' village, where Randolph had started to play with an axe. Nobody meant to hurt Mac, Jessie thought. Of course they didn't. But when Sarah took the axe away from Randolph and threw it at the wood-pile, it struck something. The head came off—and flew straight toward Mac as he slept in Jessie's lap.

Luckily she was ten years old, and strong enough to ward it off so it hit Mac with the blunt edge instead of the sharp one. But even so, it had cut Mac's head, and bruised her arm, too. Big sister Eliza had been too frightened to move. Nobody was there to take charge. So Jessie had called Wesley and told him to carry Mac to the Big House.

When they came to the brook, the children stopped to give Mac a drink. "Mother—Mother!" he faintly wailed as he lay on the ground.

Here, where the lane made a long loop away from the Big House, they generally took a short cut. But to-day a great, grayish-brown bull stood in the meadow, head up, watching.

Jessie looked at him—and the long lane—and Mac's bleeding head. "Through the meadow! Hurry!" she urged.

However, Wesley insisted that the lane would be safer, and no matter how Jessie coaxed, he refused to run the risk. So she gathered Mac up in her left arm, the uninjured one, and clambered over the rails.

Slowly the bull moved toward her. Slowly she backed away, stepping softly—softly—keeping the brook between them. After what seemed a long time she reached the opposite fence, boosted Mac through the rails, and scrambled across. Then, bursting into tears, she picked up the little boy and ran the rest of the way.

Her mother was upstairs with one of the many aunts who were also visiting Cherry Grove. Too breathless to speak, Jessie rushed through the bedroom door and laid the bloody child on her knees. Her mother was silent, but the aunt, taking one look at Jessie's bloodstained clothes, jumped to a conclusion.

"Jessie has killed her little brother!" she exclaimed.

To Jessie's horror, her mother seemed to believe it. "Go away!" was all she said.

Jessie couldn't believe her ears. How could her mother, her very own mother, think she had hit poor little Mac? If only her father were there! He would never, never for a moment, believe she could hurt their sick little boy. He would put his arms around her and ask how it happened and give her a chance to explain. Sobbing, she ran to her room to cry herself to sleep.

Much later Grandmother McDowell gently awakened her. "Mac wasn't much hurt," she said. "He's already playing around, with a bandage on his head. And, Jessie—Wesley came in right after you did and told us what happened. You were a brave girl."

So Jessie was a heroine after all. Her father sent her a special book with a long letter, all about gladiators and lions. Even Grandfather, who usually thought she was too noisy and too bouncy, laid his long, thin hands on her head, saying, "I'm pleased with you, for you've been a brave child."

It was all right after all, Jessie decided, even though her arm was sore for a long time. Saving Mac had been the main thing.

Slave quarters on a plantation in the South, similar to those at Cherry Grove. (Courtesy of the New York Historical Society, New York City.)

CHERRY GROVE was only one of Jessie's homes. She had two others which she visited by turns because her father—Thomas Hart Benton—was a United States senator. In winter, while the Senate was in session, the Benton family lived in Washington, D.C., but in the summer they visited relatives. Every even-numbered year they went to Cherry Grove, where Jessie's mother had grown up as a southern belle. Jessie herself had been born there on May 31, 1824.

The trip to Cherry Grove was exciting. It started by stagecoach, but at Fredericksburg, Virginia, the family was met by Grandfather McDowell riding a fine horse, and by the huge, high, bright yellow McDowell traveling coach—"Cinderella's pumpkin," the children called it. Then, after visiting several cousins, they swept up a long lane bordered by cherry trees to the high-pillared white house, where Grandmother McDowell rushed out, laughing and crying and trying to hug everybody at once.

The house was full of relatives, so many that at morning prayers they overflowed from the library into the hall. After prayers, Jessie could race with her laughing cousins up dusty stairs to the attic, to try on lavender-scented dresses of forgotten ancestors. They played charades, put on plays, visited the workers' village to watch the blacksmith and weavers and carpenters. These servants were slaves, for it was long before the Civil War. But Jessie's parents abhorred slavery, and in their Washington home all the servants were free.

Although Jessie's father was away most of the summer campaigning for the Democratic party, he came to Cherry Grove in the fall, and then Jessie followed him "like a pet doggie," for she loved him dearly. A tall, emphatic man with red hair and lively blue eyes, he read to her, and sometimes took her hunting in the sunny hills. For Jessie, these were the best times of all.

And then, in a flash, the Cherry Grove summer was gone. While Grandmother cried, Jessie and her family once more climbed aboard "Cinderella's pumpkin" to go back to Washington, D.C.

The other years, the odd-numbered ones, Congress recessed earlier, so they had time to make the much longer trip to St. Louis, Missouri, where her father's relatives lived. He was a senator from that state, and its leading citizen.

St. Louis was on the Mississippi River, in the westernmost state, with a vast, lonely wilderness of Indians and buffalo beyond. Jessie loved the two weeks' trip—the prancing fresh horses at the stagecoach stops, the breeze and the sunshine. Her father, who often rode outside on the box, let her sit there too while he told stories of covered wagons, blizzards, accidents and highwaymen.

At the Ohio River they changed to a steamboat that took them to St. Louis, the home of Grandmother Benton, a crippled old lady in black. Timidly Jessie would walk into Grandmother's room and receive a kiss from her dry old lips.

"Stay out in the sunshine and keep your rosy cheeks," this grandmother always said, because her husband and several children had died young of tuberculosis—"consumption" they called it then. This was the disease Mac had.

Summers in St. Louis were hot, robust and jolly. The city had been founded long ago by French furtraders, and it still seemed more French than American. Jessie saw peasant women in wooden shoes and white caps, trappers in fringed buckskins, and long files of Indians who stepped silently along. On levees by the river she could hear black boat-hands singing quick, wild songs as they loaded the puffing steamers, or she could walk past the village of Indian teepees just outside the town. All day she chattered in French with her friends. She also took Spanish lessons from an old army

*View of Cairo, Illinois, in 1838, by Mendelli. This is
the Mississippi River as Jessie saw it when she traveled
by steamboat to St. Louis. (Courtesy of the St. Louis
Art Museum. Gift of Joseph Verner Reed, Jersey City,
New Jersey.)*

officer, because her father wanted his children to learn
the "neighbor language."

Jessie liked all the week except Sundays. Her
mother belonged to the Presbyterian Church, which,
like other churches at that time, was very strict. The
dull hours began on Saturday, when the children had to
study their Sunday school lesson. On the "Lord's Day"

they couldn't play, or read any books except religious ones. They had to attend two long services in a barnlike building. But their French playmates went to a Catholic church that was lighted with candles and fragrant with incense, and after mass they had a holiday.

One Saturday when her mother was away, Jessie ran to the home of a friend. "I can stay all night!" she exclaimed, so happily that the friend's mother thought she had permission.

View of Front Street, St. Louis, 1840, by J. H. Wild. Jessie visited this city many times. (Courtesy of the Missouri Historical Society, St. Louis. Negative #—Public Buildings 26.)

Freedom was sweet but brief, for at sundown the French governess was sent to bring her home in disgrace.

"Why did you go visiting without permission?" demanded her mother. "Why did you neglect to study your Sunday school lesson?"

"I wanted to go to mass!" Jessie stormed. "I hate the Presbyterian Church—no flowers, no candlelight, no pictures."

Her mother was shocked. Sternly she sent Jessie to her room to wait for her father, who came in softly, and talked with her a long time behind closed doors.

That night, while they were getting ready for bed, her sister Eliza whispered, "What did Father say?"

Jessie, who was brushing her red-brown curls, paused, brush in hand. "He scolded me for disrespect to Mother," she whispered back. "But not to the Presbyterians."

As always, her father understood just how she felt.

St. Louis was fun. Cherry Grove was enchanting. But these were for summers, for vacations, for playing with cousins and easy, carefree times. Jessie had still another place to live, and it was the best of all.

"You may have several houses but only one ever feels *home*," she once said.

It was in Washington, D.C., that the greatest adventures began.

Jessie Cuts Her Hair

1824-1838

IN WINTER, when Jessie lived in Washington, D.C., the center of her life was her red-haired father. Because her mother was not very well, the senator was really in charge, and the children adored him.

He had strong and sometimes peculiar ideas. Any child who spoke of a disagreeable topic during dinner had to eat the next meal alone. Because he feared consumption, he had the children play outside every day, even in snow or rain, and they must stand before open windows for breathing exercises. But even this didn't save little Mac, who died when he was five.

Washington then was a rough new city. Thieves carried knives along dimly lighted streets, and creeks smelled like sewage because indoor plumbing was unknown. However, the Capitol and White House were handsome buildings, and some of the homes on Capitol Hill were mansions.

The Bentons lived in one of these, a brick house of

high-ceilinged rooms where the children romped on shining oak floors, or warmed themselves beside crackling fireplaces. Instead of going to school, they studied with tutors. Jessie was lonely, because Eliza was frail and the rest—including the new baby, Susan—were much younger. So she was often with her father.

"Come in," he would say if she tapped at his study door. "But you must be as quiet as a little mouse."

The study was her favorite room, large and quiet, with bookshelves all the way to the ceiling. She would

The Capitol in 1837, before its dome and wings were added. (Courtesy of the Library of Congress.)

lie on the floor for hours, looking at pictures, while the senator and his friends talked about the nation's business. To Jessie it seemed only natural to hear about laws and courts and elections.

In Washington, just as in St. Louis and Cherry Grove, she was frequently in trouble, for she had a way of acting first and thinking afterward. Once when she was five, she and Eliza wandered into the study, where a fresh copy of a speech lay on the desk, with a box of blue and red pencils nearby. Gleefully Jessie clambered up to the desk and began to "write" with a red pencil, while timid Eliza followed her lead, with blue. Soon they were sprawled on the floor, covering the manuscript with great zigzags of color. Their brand-new purple velvet coats were smeared, and so were their faces.

Suddenly they heard a roar from their astonished father who was standing in the doorway. "Who did this?" he demanded.

While Eliza wept, Jessie scrambled to her feet. "Do you really want to know?" she asked.

"Of course."

"Oh." Jessie thought fast. She had often heard campaign slogans about their friend President Jackson, and she knew how her father loved politics. So she put on a beaming smile and exclaimed, "A little girl that cries, 'Hurrah for Jackson!' "

At this her father began to laugh and caught her up in his arms. "Don't you see, you have given me a great deal of trouble?" he said. "Go along now, and wash those faces." As usual, Jessie had gotten herself into a predicament—and out again.

Crowd rushing to the White House for the reception after President Andrew Jackson was inaugurated. This was 1829, when Jessie was not quite five years old, and Jackson was a special friend of the Benton family. (Courtesy of the Library of Congress.)

Even though she was so full of mischief, she was tender-hearted and loving. Once, when she had attended a concert at an orphanage, she exclaimed, "Oh, Father, I didn't know there were that many orphans in the whole world. Surely there can't be love enough to go round in such a place."

She was also sensitive. After finding the body of a small bird on a flower-strewn lawn, she said, "When I die, don't bury me in a box. Lay me in a bed of violets, for I want the flowers to grow up through my bones."

Living in Washington, she sometimes saw slaves being driven along the streets in chains—a sight she would never forget. Some day, she thought, she might have a chance to do something about it.

As Jessie grew older, she met many important people—men in stiff high collars, women in ruffles and hoop skirts. Since their mother was not strong, Jessie and Eliza often helped entertain senators, judges, diplomats and generals.

Slender, graceful, Jessie became a beauty, with an oval face, enormous dark eyes and curly red-brown hair. By the time she was fourteen, she had received two proposals of marriage, which so alarmed her parents that they decided to send her and Eliza to Miss English's Select Academy, a boarding school for girls, where they would live for months at a time, and—presumably—learn to behave like ladies.

Eliza, who was well by now, had friends there so she was quite willing to go. But Jessie exploded. Miss English's Academy! Prim and proper, of course, and dull as dull! It would be just like going to prison! Even though it was only three miles away, in Georgetown, it would mean leaving her father and his library crammed with books. She was sure she could learn far more studying at home, as she had always done. She begged, coaxed, wept and pleaded—to no avail. Her father said it was all decided, kissed her good night, and sent her to bed.

*Jessie's father as a young man.
(From* Memoirs of My Life, *by
John Charles Frémont, 1887.)*

There she spent the night in tears, and the next morning she ate almost nothing for breakfast, then slipped back to her room with the largest shears she could find.

Snip!

A long curl came free, to lie shining across her lap. People had always admired her hair, but now all that would be over.

Snip!

She rubbed exploring fingers across the stubble at the back of her neck. Surely, when her father saw her shock-headed like a boy, he would realize that he couldn't send her away to a place where she could never, never be happy.

The shears clicked until Jessie had shorn all her curls, and she turned her head back and forth, trying out the airy, empty feeling around her shoulders. None of the girls she knew had hair cut short. She guessed it would make people laugh and whisper behind their hands. She guessed it would take years to grow again. And her father—surely he would be ashamed to have her go to school looking like this.

Soon afterward, when she walked into his study, he glanced up and saw her, eyes red and swollen, hair cut to a brush of jagged ends.

"Jessie!" he exclaimed. "All the other girls—what will they think?"

"I won't need other girls," she replied in a doleful voice, as she visualized herself declining into a long, lonely future. "I mean to have no more society, just to study here and be my father's companion."

Soberly the senator looked at his beautiful daughter, marred now, for in that day masses of long hair were considered a woman's "crowning glory." Much as he loved her, much as he wanted her to be happy, he was certain she needed discipline.

"You must go," he repeated.

Therefore, in the fall Jessie climbed into the family carriage beside Eliza, to watch through tears as the boxes and bags were loaded.

Like it or not, she was on her way. And since she was Jessie, something was sure to happen.

THREE

A Rebel Meets
a Handsome Hero
1838-1841

MISS ENGLISH'S ACADEMY was almost as bad as Jessie had expected, for most of the girls chattered, giggled, and followed along like so many sheep, doing exactly as the teachers told them to. Worse, the Benton sisters were supposed to do the same.

"Flat and unprofitable," Jessie called the school, and said, "I didn't study much. Really I learned nothing there."

Still, she found friends. She and a girl named Annie spent blissful hours perched in a mulberry tree, whispering, long skirts tucked around their knees, having such fun that they frequently cut classes. But one unlucky day a teacher heard stifled giggles from the mulberry leaves and hauled the culprits before the headmistress. The treetop secrets were over.

In the spring Jessie got into a "snarl," this time due to a blonde, good-natured girl named Harriet Beall Williams, who was very popular. In April she ran for May Queen with Jessie as her manager. Jessie liked politics; she knew how to campaign—and they won.

However, their triumph was brief. At the next student assembly Miss English announced that Harriet was not a good enough student, and brought forward a girl whom she called "more worthy of the honor."

Jessie was outraged. Harriet, her friend, whom everybody liked, had won the election fairly. Why bother to vote, if the results could be thrown out? Besides, this new girl couldn't even dance! While most students sat in dejected silence, Jessie raised her hand, then spoke out with a blistering opinion of the switch.

Everyone gasped. "You have a fever, Miss Jessie Benton," one teacher—Jessie called her "snaky"—said. "You will go to the infirmary and take a dose of senna."

"Blind mad," Jessie had to obey. But afterward the students rallied on the playground, "swore loyalty to our Beauty," and, led by Jessie, planned a revenge. When May Day came, instead of going to the fete, one after another reported a headache. Even though the teachers marched them off to the infirmary for the usual doses of vile-tasting senna tea, Jessie was happy, for they had spoiled the celebration.

As for Harriet, she didn't care. "It will make my father so angry that he will take me out of school," she said, smiling. "For a while, anyway, I'll have a holiday." Perhaps she knew, even then, what a splendid holiday she was to have.

*Frederick Female Seminary at Frederick City,
Maryland, about the time Jessie was at Miss English's
Select Academy. Schools like these tried to turn out
well-bred young ladies who could take their places in
polite society. (Courtesy of the Library of Congress)*

Before long everybody knew it. Sixteen-year-old
Harriet was to marry a Russian count! And Jessie was
to be the first bridesmaid.

Harriet's bridegroom was Count Alexander de la
Bodisco, the Ambassador from Russia. "Bodisco the
Splendid," Jessie called him, because of his snow-white

carriage drawn by prancing black horses. Still, she was disappointed, for although Bodisco was kind and wealthy, he was sixty-one years old, with a broad wrinkled face, shaggy whiskers, and projecting teeth.

Even so, by the day of the wedding she was beside herself with excitement, for she was to stay up far later than her usual nine o'clock bedtime, wear a white satin dress with a low neck, and carry a feather fan. All the men in the party were to be elderly diplomats like the count, while the bridesmaids would be young and pretty. Jessie's partner was James Buchanan, Senator from Pennsylvania.

On the wedding day the young attendants gathered at the bride's home, with Harriet splendid in a white satin dress, veil of silver lace, and coronet of red velvet covered with diamonds. Outside, a crowd overflowed into the piazzas and grounds. All the diplomatic corps were there in full dress, army and navy officers in uniform, ladies in ruffles and silk, and even President Van Buren.

"What a dazzle!" Jessie exclaimed.

Gleefully the bridesmaids peeped between the blinds. "Girls! Here comes the count's carriage!" exclaimed Harriet. "See the satin rosettes on the horses!"

After the ceremony, carriages took them to the Russian embassy to spend the day in celebration. For emotional, fourteen-year-old Jessie it was almost more than she could bear, and by evening she had a violent headache. It was time, her father said, to go back to school.

This was intolerable, thought Jessie, but as before, her tears were of no avail. Once again she climbed into a carriage and set out for the detested academy.

One evening of the next spring, when her sister Sarah came to the school for a concert, Jessie rushed into the visitors' room to meet her. But this time she stopped in surprise, for beside Sarah stood a smiling young stranger in army uniform.

Bridal party at the Bodisco wedding. Jessie, the bridesmaid nearest the bride, is standing between two "gentlemen," with her hands clasped. (From Souvenirs of My Time, *by Jessie Benton Frémont, 1887.)*

"Lieutenant Frémont," Sarah murmured, and explained that he had brought her because her parents were busy.

Bending his dark head, the officer raised Jessie's hand to his lips. He was not very tall, slender, with a soldier's erect bearing.

At the concert, where he sat beside Jessie, neither one said much as they pretended to listen to the music. She peeped at him occasionally—how tanned he was! What intelligent, deep blue eyes! Such dark, curly hair! How nicely he could smile!

That night she confided to Eliza, "I've met the handsomest man in Washington. I'm *so* glad I wore the pink candy-stripe satin with the rose sash, instead of the dotted muslin with blue. It made me look much older!"

She didn't know it, but Frémont went home in a daze, thinking only of Jessie's soft brown eyes, her bright curls, the pure oval of her face and sparkling smile.

"I've fallen in love at first sight," he told a friend. "My one thought is how and where I may meet Miss Jessie again." He said she was like a rose, like a beautiful picture, and that "there came a glow into my heart which changed the current and color of daily life and gave beauty to common things."

This young man was John Charles Frémont, second lieutenant in the United States Topographical Corps, and recently returned from an expedition to the Mississippi River. There he had done so well that when they

The earliest known picture of John Charles Frémont, made about the time he met Jessie, and before he grew a beard. (From an early edition of his report on his first expedition, by John Charles Frémont, 1843.)

returned, he had been invited to room with its leader, Joseph Nicolas Nicollet, in Washington, and help write the official report.

Inevitably Frémont had met Senator Benton, who was fascinated with the West. Throughout that winter he had been a frequent dinner guest in the Benton home, and when Sarah needed an escort, he had volunteered.

During the next months the lieutenant and Jessie saw each other only occasionally, when she went home to visit and he was a dinner guest. Then he watched as she assisted her mother, and she was fascinated by his explorer tales. They began to snatch moments alone and arranged a way to exchange letters. Summer passed. By the next spring sixteen-year-old Jessie and twenty-seven-year-old Frémont were so openly in love that her parents were alarmed.

They called her to the library. "We all admire Lieutenant Frémont, but with no family, no money, and the prospects of slow promotion in the army, we think him no proper match for you," her father said. "Besides, you are too young to think of marriage."

Although Jessie didn't agree, for she considered herself a woman, she waited quietly while he continued, "You are for a time at least to see him only on rare occasions."

They also warned Frémont, and for several weeks the lovers had no chance to meet.

Then in April, 1841, only a month after his inauguration, the new President William Henry Harrison died. Immediately a note came from Lieutenant Frémont, saying that the funeral procession would pass in front of the house where he worked on his maps. He invited the Benton family to use this room, whose windows would give an excellent view.

Senator and Mrs. Benton couldn't accept, because they had to make an official appearance, but Grandmother McDowell was visiting them, and she was delighted. Since Jessie's father thought the lieutenant would be on military duty, he said she could go, too.

However, things weren't quite as the senator expected, for Frémont had claimed a slight cold and obtained a sick leave. When Jessie and her grandmother arrived, he was there, handsome in his best uniform, his blue eyes glowing with joy.

He had gone to great trouble, decorating the room with potted geraniums and roses. Flames danced in the fireplace; a table was laden with bonbons and cakes.

The funeral procession passed, with marching men, plumed white horses pulling the flag-draped hearse. While the others watched, Jessie and Frémont sat alone in a daze of happiness. He proposed marriage. She accepted, but said they must keep the engagement secret.

However, Jessie's parents soon heard about this meeting, and they frantically pulled political strings. As a result, in early June the young lieutenant received orders to abandon his report and prepare to lead an expedition to the Des Moines River, on the unexplored prairies.

Although this was a great honor for such a young man, he thought the maps he was working on were important—and Jessie was more so. He wanted to decline, and Nicollet, his superior, protested that Frémont was needed to finish the report.

"There's some deviltry here," he grumbled, shaking his head.

All was in vain. The army had made a decision, which Frémont, a soldier, had to obey.

At this news Jessie became so still and tearful that her father relented slightly, saying they might meet—once—in the home library. Further, when he saw how white and stricken she looked at the moment of farewell, he made another concession. After one year, if they were still in love, they might marry.

Jessie watched through tears as Frémont bowed low to her father and bent for the last time over her hand. A year seemed practically forever! Out there in the trackless wilderness he would be at the mercy of wild beasts, hostile Indians, raging rivers and prairie fires.

Perhaps he would never return.

FOUR

Love Never Dies

1841-1842

AFTER FREMONT LEFT, Jessie was miserable, wandering from room to room, not really interested in anything. She knew it would often be like this if she married an explorer, for he would be away for months or years at a time. And yet—his daring, his brilliance, his toughness—these were the reasons she loved him. She wouldn't change him, even if she could.

In midsummer, when a Virginia cousin was married at Cherry Grove, Jessie, Eliza and their mother attended. This meant new clothes, dances and parties, with thirty-five house guests gathered from all over the South. It was almost like the wonderful summers of long ago, and Jessie revived. She seemed so much her old self that her mother happily wrote to the senator, "I truly believe our Jessie's childish love affair has quite blown over."

Nothing could have been further from the truth. One day, when she and her favorite cousin Preston were exploring the attic, they found some letters tied with ribbons. Thoughtlessly he unfolded the crumbling paper and started to read. "Flower of my heart . . ."

Jessie snatched it away. "Would you eavesdrop if those two were here?" she asked.

"Of course not, but they are dead long ago."

"Love never dies. Let's put it back." Swiftly she retied the bundle and returned it to the trunk.

The visit which began with such joy ended with sadness. Just as the Bentons were about to leave Cherry Grove, lively little Grandmother McDowell fell ill, and in only a few days she was dead. After the funeral Eliza found Jessie in the garden, lying behind a row of phlox and weeping.

"Don't grieve so," Eliza murmured, taking her in her arms. "Grandmother was old, and hers was an easy death."

"I'm not grieving for Grandmother," Jessie said between sobs. "She was happy. My heart is breaking for my own unhappy life."

From that day, whenever the family opposed Jessie's romance, the gentle, sympathetic Eliza took her part.

When the visit was over and they returned to Washington, Jessie continued her lovesick dreams. She turned her desk into a shrine for Frémont, with burning candles in front of a newspaper picture of the hero. But she hadn't long to wait, for in the second week of August her lieutenant returned to the city and hurried at once to the Benton house. Outwardly he came to pay his

Jessie as a young girl. (From
Memoirs of My Life, *by John
Charles Frémont, 1887.)*

respects to the senator, but he was actually seeking Jessie. When Benton saw the lovers' rapturous greeting, he realized that time hadn't made a difference after all.

Nevertheless, he still opposed the match. During the next weeks, while Frémont was busy working on his report, Jessie spent very little time with him alone. But she often heard him discussed, all over the city, and she glowed with pride, for he had established the course of the Des Moines River, all the way to its source.

Since she couldn't see him openly, Jessie began to slip out of the house, saying she was going to call on young Mrs. J. J. Crittenden, whose husband was a senator. However, the real attraction was Frémont, who secretly met her at the Crittenden house.

Although Jessie longed to marry soon, her parents still insisted on the remaining half year of delay, which seemed an interminable time. The young couple was afraid that Frémont might be transferred, or sent on another expedition which would separate them for years. So they decided to act.

First, Frémont and his sponsor Nicollet visited three Protestant clergymen, trying to arrange a secret marriage. Each one refused because he feared the senator's wrath.

Next, Mrs. Crittenden, being young and romantic, searched until she found a Catholic priest who was both willing and courageous. On October 19, 1841, at the Crittenden home, Jessie and John Charles Frémont were married. She was seventeen years old, while he was twenty-eight.

Immediately afterward she returned home. Days passed. Although friends knew what they had done, Senator Benton didn't, for they were afraid to confess.

"Why don't you go, manly and open as you are, forward and put things by a single step to the right," one worried friend wrote to Frémont. "Nothing very serious *can* happen now—the prize is secured."

His sponsor Nicollet also urged them to act.

"The sooner the better," Frémont agreed. "But as to that, Mrs. Frémont [meaning Jessie herself] must decide."

They were afraid to tell—but they must. Finally he

offered to go alone to the senator, saying, "This is a matter between men."

Frightened as she was, Jessie wouldn't dodge a duty, and besides, this might be exciting. "We will explain together," she replied. "Come to the house tomorrow."

Her heart was beating fast the next morning and Frémont, the intrepid explorer, trembled as he blurted out their news. Neither he nor Jessie had expected Benton's reaction.

"Get out of the house and never cross my door again!" he bellowed, squaring his broad shoulders. "Jessie shall stay here."

But Jessie was her father's daughter, with a full share of spunk. Taking her husband's arm and moving closer to him, she repeated in a shaky but determined voice the pledge of Ruth from the Bible. "Whither thou goest I will go, and where thou lodgest, I will lodge; thy people shall be my people, and thy God my God."

For a moment Benton was astonished into silence. Then he gruffly commanded, "Go collect your belongings and return at once to the house. I will prepare Mrs. Benton."

So Frémont moved into the roomy Benton mansion, where Jessie's father grumbled at first, but soon was telling his friends that her happiness had led him to approve the marriage.

Jessie loved her new role as Frémont's wife. They were quickly accepted as the most exciting young couple in Washington. On New Year's Day when they went to a White House reception, the crowd cheered as he assisted her from the carriage. They were both in dark blue and gold, he in his best uniform, she in a velvet gown with frills of lace, a tiny cape, lemon-colored gloves, and a blue bonnet trimmed with ostrich plumes. While a vast crowd milled about in the vestibule and the military band played, she greeted the president, bowed to friends, and beamed as people congratulated her on the lieutenant's feats.

Day followed day, with dances, musicales, shopping, and always the joy of being together. Except for one thing, Jessie would have been supremely happy. That one thing was fear—the fear that her husband must leave her again. She often heard men talking in her father's study about a new exploration much farther west, and since Nicollet's health was failing, he urged the appointment of Frémont instead.

At that time a huge territory called Oregon was held jointly by Great Britain and the United States, its ownership to be decided later. People disagreed violently about it, some wanting it, while others considered it too remote to be worth the trouble.

A few trappers had already been there, a group of settlers planned to go in the summer, and more were sure to follow, but the trail hadn't been properly explored. People and animals had died on it for lack of food and water. Information was needed about Indians, distances, passes, about animals and vegetation and weather. As Jessie listened to the arguments in her father's study, she felt both pride and dread.

All too soon these were realized, for the secretary of war ordered Frémont to head an expedition to the country between the Missouri River and the Rocky Mountains. Now, thought Jessie, she would be tested. Since loneliness was the price of her marriage, she must pay it without complaint.

Although by now she was pregnant, she felt well, and for a glorious three months she lived in a whirl of excitement, with men in and out of the house at all hours, bringing ideas and plans. Full of energy, she became her husband's buffer, protecting him from inventors with fanciful gadgets, hopeful salesmen, and young adventurers who wanted to join up. He was busy buying supplies, and he designed his own expedition flag. Earlier explorers' flags had had eagles whose talons held bundles of arrows, but on this one the eagle held a peace pipe.

Only four weeks were left—three—two. As the day of departure drew near, Jessie sometimes sparkled with life, but at other times she turned pale and sad. She would have more than one explorer to worry about. Her father, longing to make the journey but not able to, decided to send twelve-year-old Randolph instead.

And then it was the last morning. Although she had planned to go to the railroad station to say farewell, her mother collapsed from the strain of parting with Randolph, so Jessie had to stay home to look after her and the weeping sisters. She helped her husband put on his new blue and gold uniform and patted the braid and buttons, determined that his last memory would be of a smiling wife. The carriage was at the door. Frémont caught her to him for a final embrace. The door closed, and the house was still.

To Jessie the loneliness and silence were torture, and when her father saw her white face and the shadows under her dark eyes, he was worried, for he truly loved this tempestuous daughter. Calling her to the library, he pointed to the end of the table and said, "I want you to resume your old place there; you are too young to fritter away your life." He said he had "a great pressure of work," and asked her to copy some important papers.

"Gladly," she replied.

When she entered the study the next day, she found six new steel pens and fifty sheets of paper. "Only three hours' work and then a long walk," her father ordered.

He had so many other ways of having papers copied that Jessie suspected this was merely a means of keeping her occupied. Nevertheless she set to with a will. She loved her father, and she loved books and ideas. They would help her keep busy and cheerful, though she wouldn't be really happy until Mr. Frémont returned. When Jessie gave her heart, she gave it without stint.

"I Trust and Go"

1842-1843

EVEN WITH HER father's papers to copy and a new baby to plan for, Jessie found the summer long and lonely. But worse was to come, for in early autumn her mother collapsed with a stroke, which left her almost helpless. Jessie's father, who had always been so strong, was inconsolable. He sat or knelt beside his wife's bed, trying to warm her cold hands in his, or he tenderly picked her up and carried her to a couch. When he could bear it no longer, he would go into another room to weep.

Emotional Jessie, who had been such a wayward child, was now the one on whom the family leaned.

"There must be only cheerful faces around your mother," the doctor warned her. "Go off to cry when you must, but always come to her smiling."

For weeks Eliza ran the house while Jessie supervised the hired nurse, comforted her father, saw that a flower was always placed on the invalid's tray, and spent hours reading aloud.

In late October her worry gave way to joy, for her husband returned, triumphant. He had reached the Rockies in his first important exploration, to be called Frémont's First Expedition. Now he must write up his report.

However, that was delayed by the birth of Jessie's baby, a little girl, on November 13, 1842. Although she had wanted a boy, the disappointment didn't last long, and she tenderly loved this tiny creature. When the senator suggested naming the baby Elizabeth, for Jessie's mother, the young parents agreed. But they always called her Lily.

The day after Lily's birth Frémont proudly tiptoed into Jessie's bedroom carrying a thick bundle.

"This flag was raised over the highest peak of the Rocky Mountains; I brought it to you," he said, as he gently spread it over her bed. It was the Rocky Mountain flag, the one with the eagle and peace pipe. Happy to have it, and happier still because her husband was safe, Jessie stroked the faded stripes.

Soon she was strong enough to enjoy the glowing newspaper stories about her romantic young husband. When, they asked, would his official report be released? People were waiting for it. Having heard his enthralling tales, Jessie was sure it would be the finest report ever. Smiling, she supplied ink, paper and pens, and waited for the first pages.

However, Frémont dipped the pen, wrote a few

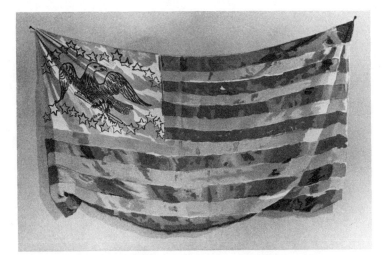

The flag that Frémont carried on his first expedition.
He brought it home and laid it over Jessie's bed. (From Memoirs of My Life, *by John Charles Frémont, 1887.)*

lines—and crumpled the sheet. He tried again. For three days the wastebasket overflowed, with nothing accomplished. On the fourth day he had a severe headache and nosebleed—and gave up.

Jessie didn't hesitate. Perhaps her husband couldn't write his report, but he could tell it, and she could wield the pen. As she said, "The horseback life, the sleep in the open air, had unfitted Mr. Frémont for the indoor work of writing—and second lieutenants cannot indulge in secretaries. I was let to try, and thus slid into my most happy life work." Here, and always, she called her husband by his title, as most women did in her day.

Now, working with her "Mr. Frémont," she was indeed happy. Every morning at nine o'clock she took her seat, writing like mad to keep up while he paced

A buffalo hunt on Frémont's first expedition. Jessie learned about scenes such as this while she was helping her young husband write his report. (From Memoirs of My Life, *by John Charles Frémont, 1887.)*

back and forth and dictated. When he faltered, she prompted him by eager questions. Sometimes it was hard, for if she made a single restless motion, he would come to a stammering halt, and so she must sit still as a stone, except for her scratching pen. But she felt only "the great joy of being so useful to him."

As they worked, she lived it all. She met Kit Carson, the famous mountain man who had become Frémont's right-hand aide. She thrilled to the buffalo hunt, Indian threats, dangerous rapids. And sparked by her interest, he spoke vividly, as when he described clinging to ledges of a perilous bluff, or said, "Indians and buffalo were the poetry and life of the prairie."

When the little book of 120 pages was complete, Jessie turned toward him. "I have not put to paper one-half the beauty and truth you have shown me, but I have done the best I could, my darling," she said. She was almost sorry to have finished.

Jessie didn't write this report—she transcribed it. However, without her help, it would have been less interesting, and therefore less influential. It was the first published work on the West to give accurate and readable information. Printed for Congress, with one thousand extra copies for the public, it was widely copied, for it described the soil, climate, geology, and Indians. Most important, it said the plains were not dry desert, as had been thought, but were fertile, with ample woods and prairies. All this encouraged emigration.

Even before it was finished, Frémont was asked to lead another expedition, this time all the way to the west coast. Outwardly he would only map the trail, but privately his backers wanted to promote American ownership of the land beyond the Rockies.

Frémont himself later wrote, "The object of this expedition was not merely a survey; beyond that was its bearing on the holding of our territory on the Pacific."

On March 10, 1843, he received an official appointment to lead this, his second expedition, and as soon as possible the whole family, including the baby and the invalid mother, went to St. Louis, by what Jessie called "our creep-mouse rate of travel." There Mr. Frémont finished his preparations, while Jessie spent a blissful week as his secretary.

Along with other ammunition he ordered a twelve-pound cannon, which he promptly received. However, the captain at the St. Louis Arsenal, who issued it, wrote to Washington to say he didn't approve. Neither Jessie nor Frémont knew about this letter, and even if they had, they wouldn't have worried about it then.

As soon as he could, Frémont pushed on to a camp near Westport Landing (now Kansas City) to finish preparations, leaving Jessie in St. Louis. She was to read his mail, forwarding only the most important.

A few days later she went for a long walk through streets that were fragrant with jasmine and locust blossoms. She could hear black workmen on the levee, singing as they loaded the steamboats, and the clank and rattle of westward-bound carts.

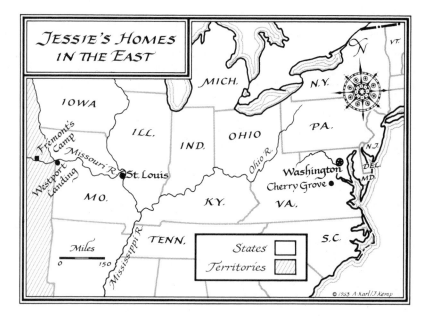

When she returned, she found a pile of mail, topped by a long, official envelope. As Mr. Frémont had asked, she tore it open—and gasped. The letter from the Captain of the Arsenal had done its mischief. Colonel John J. Abert of the Bureau of Engineers, who had received it, was questioning the use of a cannon on a peaceful survey. He ordered Frémont to return to Washington and explain, saying that another officer would have charge of the men during his absence.

Jessie was horrified. His fine, picked men under an ordinary officer! Her lieutenant might lose his chance of a lifetime!

"I was only eighteen, an age when one takes risks willingly," she wrote later. "I felt the whole situation in a flash, and met it—as *I* saw right!"

She alone could act! She would destroy the letter! But suppose a duplicate had been sent! Her Mr. Frémont must leave camp at once, before word could possibly find him. Then he would be out of reach, and if he disobeyed the order, he would be blameless.

Trembling, she sent for a French Canadian named de Rosier, who was planning to join the expedition in a few days.

"An important letter has come for Lieutenant Frémont, and I want it delivered without loss of time," she told de Rosier. "How long will you need to get ready?"

"The time to get my horse."

"Say nothing of this, de Rosier," she then said. "But you, going by land, can cut off the bends in the river, and save the time the mail boat will lose by night on account of the river fogs.

De Rosier agreed that he could outrun the boat, and suggested taking his brother along. "Two horses travel together better, and he will bring back an answer," he said.

Pleased, Jessie sat down at her desk, not to forward the letter, but to write one of her own. "Do not lose a day, but start at once," she wrote. "I cannot tell you the reason, but you must GO. Only trust me and go." Handing it to de Rosier, she saw him off on the four-hundred mile ride.

For a whole week she waited, wondering whether she had been in time. At last, one warm day, the messenger's brother knocked at the door and handed her a note.

"Goodbye," it said. "I trust and go."

As Jessie read it, her spirits rose, for her husband was safely on his way. But through her he was disobeying military orders—and he was a soldier. She had taken a big risk.

Gabriel Sees a Ghost

1843-1844

AS SOON as Jessie knew that her husband was started, she wrote to the colonel who had sent the order, for she didn't intend to dodge blame. She suggested that he must have acted without knowing all the facts; that if Frémont had gone to Washington, it would have delayed the expedition; that he had to leave early or lose the best spring grass; and that he needed the cannon to impress the tribes. She said she had withheld the order because she knew that if her husband received it, he would have to obey, which would have been a grave mistake.

Once her explanation was in the mail, she was almost overcome by fear that she had done harm. However, although she received no reply, Colonel Abert didn't appear to feel any resentment. For the time being, at least, Frémont's career was undamaged.

Now Jessie settled back for a long wait, probably

The city of St. Louis, seen from across the Mississippi River, during the early years of Jessie's marriage. (From Frémont and '49, *by Frederick S. Dellenbaugh, 1914.)*

nine months without even a letter. This time she was to spend it in her father's St. Louis home.

The city was busy, that summer of 1843, the year of the first large migration to Oregon. Wagons rumbled through the streets and mounds of supplies stood on the board walks. The quiet French town was being transformed by hustling Americans, for it was the gateway to the West. But Jessie still had many relatives and friends there who made it seem like home.

In early fall Senator Benton returned to Washington, while Jessie stayed on in St. Louis. Sometimes she walked to the emigrant camp just outside of town, where caravans of covered wagons were waiting to start down the trail. One day she stopped to talk with a young woman in a pink sunbonnet.

"Wouldn't you and your folks like to come along?" the young woman asked. "There are three wagons of us. Did you know you can get a whole section of good land to yourselves and save your children from a life of wages?"

"I can't go because of my sick mother. But how I wish I could," Jessie replied, not explaining that she was a senator's daughter and a famous explorer's wife. As she walked quickly on, tears were streaming down her face. All of them, the emigrant wives, could go with their husbands. She was the unlucky one who had to stay behind.

"If it weren't for mother," she wrote to her father that evening, "I would take Lily and go with them. I am strong, and not afraid, and waiting grows harder every day."

In late autumn she was overjoyed to hear through messengers that Frémont and his men were safe, and had left Oregon. This was marvelous news. Even though he planned to return by way of California, he would surely be back by March, perhaps even sooner.

All through Christmas Jessie hugged the thought that Mr. Frémont was on his way home. Her father came for the holidays, and her mother was somewhat better, although her speech was still jumbled. Eliza was there, along with many other relatives who were in and out of the house. Besides the usual Yule log and roast goose, Jessie had the fun of trimming a Christmas tree for Lily—a new custom, brought to America by German settlers.

By February, with her husband due soon, Jessie began to prepare a gala welcome. She made new clothes for herself and Lily and kept the house in perfect order. Every evening she set a table for his supper, turned down his bed, and placed a lamp in the window to burn all night. Then she lay half awake, listening to every step in the street.

May 13 came—and he had been gone a year.

Her birthday came—and she was twenty.

June passed—July—and still he had not arrived.

Jessie lost weight and turned pale and still. When her father joined them for the summer, he was appalled at her listlessness. No one told her of the rumor brought by Indians, the rumor that said Frémont had tried to cross the mountains in winter, had been caught in terrible snows, and was starving. But Jessie was sure something dreadful had happened, for she sensed it from her friends' "expressions of protecting tender friendliness."

On the evening of August 6, Jessie received word that her cousin Anne Potts's husband was dying, so she hurried to the Potts home, where she watched beside the sick man until nearly morning, then went wearily to bed. She had scarcely closed her eyes when an excited maid aroused her. Gabriel, the Benton family's black coachman, had brought word that Frémont was safe!

That he was already in the city! Jessie's heart beat fast as she threw on a robe and hurried downstairs, where she found Gabriel standing in the hall and trembling from head to foot.

"I heard gravel thrown through the window," Gabriel said, "and then I looked outside. And I saw the lieutenant in his uniform and thin as a shadow." He said Frémont had asked if everybody was well, and if he could get into the house without making a noise. "First I took it for a spirit," Gabriel said. "Then I made sure it was him and said Miss Jessie was at Miss Anne's. And then he went off quick downtown."

By now the Potts family had gathered in the hall, all of them skeptical. One said that Gabriel must be suffering from "either corn whiskey or a ghost." Hearing the word "ghost," the family nurse decided the lieutenant was dead and burst into loud wails. Even Gabriel, faced by so many doubters, was none too sure whether he had seen a living man, or a spirit, or had only been dreaming.

In the midst of the confusion, while Gabriel was still scratching his bewildered head, the door opened to admit the lieutenant himself, tired, thin, but definitely not a ghost. Laughing and crying, Jessie flung herself into his arms, and as soon as everyone was calm enough, Frémont explained.

He had come late the night before. Not wanting to arouse the family, he had thrown pebbles at Gabriel's window. When Gabriel said that Jessie had gone to the Potts's home, Frémont first thought of following her.

Frémont, the young explorer. A daguerrotype by Matthew Brady, made after the second expedition. (From Frémont the West's Greatest Adventurer, *by Allan Nevins. Published by Harper and Row, 1928.)*

Then, rather than disturb a sick man in the night, he had decided to wait on the lawn of Barnum's Hotel. An employee, seeing him there, had offered him a bed; he had gratefully accepted, had fallen sound asleep, and had just awakened. So here he was, alive and well.

Almost at once a crowd of well-wishers began to gather, for he was famous, and word of his return spread fast. Instead of having him to herself, as she longed to do, Jessie was plunged into an impromptu reception. People were excited because he had not only gone to the Oregon country, but had entered California, where American settlers were beginning to resent Mexican rule. Jessie's heart was proud as she watched him, slim and assured, answering their eager questions.

No matter that she must share him and wait for their quiet time alone. Her explorer had come back. That was enough for now.

Disaster

1844-1848

JESSIE WAS blissfully content. "Despite his appalling hardships, Lieutenant Frémont is well and handsomer than ever," she wrote to her father. "Lily is loving him as though she remembered him. Admiring friends fill the house day and night. As for me, my happiness is at times almost more than my heart can bear."

After a few days the Frémonts returned East, where, just as in St. Louis, so many visitors came that Jessie and her husband couldn't write his report. In desperation they finally rented a cottage just a block away, in which they could work in peace.

From nine o'clock until noon Frémont paced back and forth while he dictated, and as before, Jessie set her pen flying. Every day at one o'clock the black servant, Nancy, accompanied by two-year-old Lily, brought a basket of cold chicken and fruit, after which they took a long walk. It was a time of such peace and joy that Jessie always remembered it as "the happy winter." "It seems now that there was never any bad weather," she said.

In five months, when the report was done, Frémont proudly presented it to Congress, hoping that again a thousand copies might be printed. Instead there were ten thousand, which wasn't enough, for it was also published as a book and in newspapers and magazines.

"Frémont has returned with a name that goes over Europe and America," General Winfield Scott declared, promoting him to captain. Frémont was a national hero.

Even before finishing the report, he was told to set up his third expedition, again to the Oregon country, with secret orders to do whatever he could to secure California. As before, Jessie helped him prepare, but she also found absorbing work of her own. Secretary of State James Buchanan—the same Buchanan who had stood beside her at the Bodisco wedding—couldn't speak Spanish and didn't trust his interpreter, so he asked her to translate a confidential letter from Monterey, in California. Soon she was handling all his Mexican correspondence, a special satisfaction because it dealt with the Southwest, where her husband was soon to go.

But no matter how busy she was, the leave-taking was hard, for he had been home only nine months. On their last evening she began to cry, letting tears splash on a small leather case she had made.

"There!" she exclaimed, wiping her eyes. "That's properly dedicated, and I must be willing to dedicate you to this service which fits you. My work is to let you go cheerfully."

The next morning, when he took her into his arms for the last embrace, she was able to smile. It was May, 1845, and Jessie was not quite twenty-one.

With Mr. Frémont gone, the hours seemed long. However, she was still the tender-hearted girl who had wept over a dead bird. One day she heard about a French Canadian named Alexis Ayot, who had been crippled while on Frémont's First Expedition. He wasn't receiving a pension because he hadn't formally enlisted, and now, without funds, he said he must *mourir de faim* (die of hunger).

Although Jessie had no authority of her own, she saw that his story reached the right ears, telling it so warmly that he received not only the pension, but also two years of back pay. He came to her, swaying on his crutches, tears streaming down his dark, thin face.

"I cannot kneel to you," he said. "I have no more legs. But you are my *Sainte Madonne*. I will remember you in my prayers."

As months passed, the papers Jessie translated grew more and more exciting. War with Mexico began over the annexation of Texas to the United States. California was in ferment. An official messenger was sent to Jessie's husband with instructions so secret he had memorized and destroyed them. Frémont reached California. He egged on the rebellious American settlers. And then, one joyful day, Jessie read that he was made lieutenant-colonel, and governor and commander in chief of California.

Jessie was jubilant. "I am sorry that I could not be

the first to call you Colonel," she wrote on one of her few chances to send a letter. "Almost all of the old officers called to congratulate me upon it." She ended, "Farewell, dear, dear husband. In a few months we shall not know what sorrow means."

But before long, in translating a letter from Monterey, she read about a clash between army and navy officers there, and her heart plummeted at one dreadful sentence. "This will in all likelihood result in the removal of Colonel Frémont as commandant."

Could it be true? Jessie asked, showing it to her father. Surely, she thought, surely the senator would tell her not to worry.

Instead he gravely explained that for some time there had been trouble between General Kearny, who was commanding the army in California, and Commodore Stockton, the naval officer who had appointed Frémont as governor. The army had told the general to set up a government. The navy had told the admiral to do the same. Neither had been placed clearly in charge; they had quarreled—and Jessie's husband was the victim. All her bright hopes were dashed.

One day she had an unexpected visitor, Kit Carson, who had gone on several of Frémont's expeditions. Kit was broad-shouldered, sun-browned, with steady blue eyes. Uneasy in his ill-fitting suit of town clothes, he said "bar" for bear, "Injun" for Indian, and he made remarks like "with a good shootin-arn" he wasn't "afeared nohow."

Jessie listened, spellbound, while Kit related the

Kit Carson, Frémont's friend and aide. (From Memoirs of My Life, *by John Charles Frémont, 1887.)*

whole sorry story—that Admiral Stockton, who had been there first, had appointed Frémont as governor; that when Kearny came, his orders were different; that when these two officers quarreled, it was impossible to obey them both, or to know which was right. A cautious man, or a good politician, might have accepted orders from his superior officer, as a matter of prudence. Frémont, however, had defied General Kearny—and he was in the army. It might be considered mutiny.

Before Kit left, Jessie gave him a small oval portrait for her husband. "I am sending you myself—in miniature," she wrote. "I lay with it over my heart last night. I pray you wear it over yours until the good times return."

After that, waiting was torture. Her father said that during the day she seemed tranquil, but in the

The miniature that Kit Carson carried across the plains to Frémont, in California. It was painted in 1845, when Jessie was twenty-one years old. (From Recollections of Elizabeth Benton Frémont, *by Elizabeth Benton Frémont, 1912.)*

night she was "confused and frantic—the heart bursting, the brain burning, the body shivering." He was often called in to calm her.

In the spring, when Mr. Frémont had been gone for a little more than two years, word came, first that he was on his way home, and then that he was under arrest. This was incredible! Jessie thought. She was sure he needed her, and she needed to see him, too, as quickly as possible. So she made the long trip to St. Louis and up the Missouri River to Westport Landing.

There she stayed in a log cabin, stifling hot, until she heard the trampling of many horses. And then—he had come—he was dismounting—taking her in his arms. He looked strange in the California riding clothes of bright-colored jacket, red sash and broad-brimmed hat; his hair and beard were sprinkled with gray, face lined and weary. But he was her dear Mr. Frémont, and they were together again.

Later, one of his aides told her that General Kearny had made Frémont and his men march at the rear of the army all the way to Kansas, enveloped by dust. The general, they said, had been so hostile that they feared for their leader's life.

"But now," one of them added, "we have seen the colonel safe home—we would not trust him with Kearny. The prairies were free and we came along to watch over the colonel—he's safe now."

Safe! thought Jessie. Being under arrest? Was that safety?

Sadly, she boarded a steamboat with him, but the

journey downriver to St. Louis turned into a triumphal procession. At every wharf a crowd pressed forward, eager for a glimpse of the hero.

"Frémont! Frémont!" the cries rang out. And often, "Jessie!" There's Jessie!"

Reaching St. Louis, they took a train for Washington. Although the long years of waiting were over, it was a bittersweet journey, shadowed by fear.

Mr. Frémont was going to be tried by court-martial.

EIGHT

Court-Martial

1848-1849

IN WASHINGTON the whole family plunged into work for the trial. Jessie spent hours copying briefs and writing letters. Frémont got all his notes in order. Benton made speeches and buttonholed acquaintances.

"We shall demolish him [Kearny] with all ease and overwhelm him with disgrace," he wrote, and he told Frémont, "The enemy is now in our hands and may the Lord have mercy on them, for I feel as if I could not." He was going to be Frémont's counsel, although, being a civilian, he couldn't speak out.

In November, the first morning of the trial, Eliza suggested wearing black, but Jessie emphatically vetoed that. "No! This isn't a mourning occasion. Put on your newest dress, the blue one." She herself chose dark red with a velvet bonnet and managed a smiling face although her fingers were cold as ice.

The trial was held in the Military Arsenal, a run-down wooden building with a domed ceiling and win-

*General Stephen Watts Kearny,
commanding general in California,
who was largely responsible for
Frémont's court-martial. (Courtesy
of the Bancroft Library.)*

dows high up near the roof. Frémont and Senator Benton sat together at a side table; Kearny with his counsel sat at another. The members of the court were somber, the gold braid of their dress uniforms gleaming in the dim light. Day after day Jessie was in the audience, proudly erect, listening, fearful. Newly pregnant, she caught a severe cold, which threatened pneumonia and kept her temporarily at home, but as soon as she was well enough, she was back in her place.

This was a sensational trial, for Frémont and Jessie were both widely known and adored. Spectators thronged the courtroom.

It all seemed to go in the colonel's favor. Although the prosecution accused him of disobeying his superior, it was obvious that he had been in an impossible predicament. Even when the government had placed Kearny officially in charge, the order had come too late, and Kearny hadn't shown it to Frémont until weeks after it arrived.

The prosecution also accused him of exceeding his authority by aiding the California rebels, but the secretary of state testified that he had sent secret instructions telling him to do whatever he could to hold California.

In addition, General Kearny contradicted himself on the stand and was both forgetful and quarrelsome. One day he astonished the spectators by exploding in anger.

"When I was answering questions," he said, "the counsel of the accused, Thomas H. Benton, of Missouri, sat in his place, making mouths and grimaces at me."

This had actually happened, for Jessie's father, never a patient man, had decided that Kearny was looking "insultingly and fiendishly" at Frémont, and the senator had tried to stare the general down.

Now Benton got to his feet, and over protests of the court, he spoke out in the voice that had often shaken the Senate chambers.

Jessie's father, Senator Thomas Hart Benton. An engraving from a painting by Chappell. (From Frémont and '49, *by Frederick S. Dellenbaugh, 1914.)* Chapter Eight

"I did today look at General Kearny when he looked at Colonel Frémont," he boomed, "and I looked at him till his eyes fell—till they fell upon the floor."

Jessie was doubtful as she sat in the audience, pale, controlled, erect. Would this help her husband, or do him harm?

At last, in late January, it was over. Although most people confidently expected an acquittal, the jury found him guilty and recommended a discharge. However, they also mentioned the confusing orders and the colonel's excellent record, and recommended him to the "lenient consideration" of President Polk.

A few days later, when the president's statement finally came, it was equally cautious, calling Frémont guilty of disobedience, but innocent of mutiny. "Lieutenant-Colonel Frémont," he said, "will accordingly be released from arrest, will resume his sword, and report for duty."

It was a curious decision, seeming to say that Frémont was guilty—but not very. Almost everyone was stunned, and Jessie felt she couldn't bear it. She had been so sure her husband would be cleared, and the case had been so definite. How could the president have had any doubt?

Frémont himself was in a rage, and loudly proclaimed his innocence. Returning to the army without a full vindication, he said, would be the same as admitting guilt.

"I want justice, not official clemency," he stormed, and resigned. His pride had cost him his army career.

But before beginning his new life as a private citizen, he was to write one more report, *A Geographical Memoir Upon Upper California*, so Jessie settled down to help him with it. One important feature was the map where, for the first time, appeared the name he had given to the entrance to San Francisco Bay—"Chrysopylai," meaning "Golden Gate." He had chosen it for its shape and because he thought the harbor would receive wealth from the Orient.

Senator Benton was busy too, promoting still another expedition, to be supported not by the army but by private funds, and to search for an all-year railroad route West. Frémont was to be its leader, and whenever Jessie thought about it, she tingled with excitement, because this time she wouldn't have to wait at home.

Months before, back in California, her husband had given three thousand dollars to the consul at Monterey, with instructions to buy him a certain tract of land that was for sale on the coast. The consul had bought it—but for himself. He had then spent Frémont's money for the Mariposas, a forty-thousand-acre cattle ranch in the wild, remote Sierra Nevada Mountains, two hundred miles northeast of San Francisco. It was dry, scrubby, steep, so unsuitable for farming that Frémont at first had been furious. But he had finally decided that after this expedition he would stay in California as a rancher, and that Jessie would live there with him.

It was out of the question for her to accompany him across the continent in winter. Instead they would wait in Washington until her baby was born, then travel together to a camp on the Kansas River, where he would finish preparing the expedition. When he left camp, she and Lily and the baby would return to New York and travel from there to San Francisco.

She could take three possible routes: by covered wagon, which was much too slow and difficult; by ship around the Horn at the tip of South America, which was also slow and very dangerous; or by ship to Panama, overland across the isthmus, then by ship up the Pacific coast. Although this was by no means easy, it was the quickest and best of the three, and the one they chose.

Jessie tried not to think too much about the isthmus, which had neither canal nor railroad, but must be crossed by muleback, through country that was considered a pest-hole. Many who tried it died of Chagres fever—or malaria—or cholera—or smallpox. In some areas, anyone who stayed overnight on the land forfeited his life insurance.

None of this mattered to Jessie. For now she would stay in Washington and help her husband write his report. But soon she was going to have her own adventures.

*J*essie Rides a Mule...
and Two Ships
and a Dugout Canoe
1848-1849

"DON'T MOVE THE LAMP!" Jessie exclaimed. "It makes it too dark!"

Frémont looked at her in surprise, for nobody had touched the light by which they were working on his report. Alarmed, he moved quickly and caught her as she fainted.

For several weeks she lay extremely ill, while he labored alone on final additions to what he now called "the cursed memoir." She mended slowly, and when the baby was born, on July 24, 1848, they named him Benton, for her father, just as they had named Lily for her mother. But where Lily had been a placid, sturdy child, little Benton was frail and fretful. Worry during the trial had made her ill, Jessie thought, and the baby too.

The long, hot Washington summer passed. In September she went with her husband, six-year-old Lily, baby Benton and his nurse, to St. Louis, where she stayed with relatives while Frémont assembled his expedition. It would travel light and cross the mountains in winter, to show that it could be done.

On October 4, the explorers left St. Louis by steamboat, going to a forward camp until they finished preparations. Jessie went too, with her children, because she wanted to be with Mr. Frémont until the last possible moment. Two days later, while they were still moving up the broad Missouri River, the baby gasped—and died. His heart had been defective.

Overcome with grief, Jessie blamed the court-martial and especially General Kearny. If it hadn't been for them, she felt sure little Benton would have been healthy. However, even in the face of death, expeditions must go forward, so they moved sadly on, past Westport Landing to Boon Creek, where Jessie had a sleeping room at the home of Major Richard Cummins, the Indian agent.

Every day for eleven precious days she rode out to a large tent under the cottonwoods, to watch the final preparations. Men shouted, horses stamped, dust hung in the air. Being with her husband eased her sorrow, and the sympathetic men brought her small treats, such

Frémont's camp, which Jessie visited daily while he was finishing preparations for his fourth expedition. It is near the present site of Le Compton, Kansas. (From The Life and Public Service of John Charles Frémont, *by John Bigelow, 1856.)*

as a quail to be roasted over a fire. All too soon everything was ready, and she watched through tears as the long line moved away, with a jingle of harness and thud of hooves. Then Major Cummins took her to his house.

On the way they passed the den of a she-wolf that had been raiding sheep in order to feed her young. The night before, Cummins said, his men had found the den and killed all the cubs, so the wolf wouldn't have to hunt so much. Jessie, who had so recently lost her own child, wept in sympathy.

That night she heard the wolf howling—and dogs replying—and the prairie wind screaming around the corners of the cabin. In terror, she and the nurse built up their bedroom fire, then hung shawls over the window, for fear the animal would come to their light. The wolf was a mother too, Jessie thought, and sorrowing.

At last she drifted into troubled sleep, to be startled awake by a dark form. But it was no wolf. Mr. Frémont had ridden the five miles back from his first camp, to see her once more.

"Would Aunt Kitty [the nurse] make us tea?" he asked, and they had a final cup together. Then he rode off into the dark and rain, leaving Jessie to make the sorrowful return trip to Washington.

There two of her father's friends offered to help with her journey to California. The first was General Herron, minister from New Granada, the Spanish territory of which Panama was then a part. He gave her letters of introduction to his aunt, who lived in Panama City. The second was Henry Aspinwall, founder of a company that planned to connect the east and west coasts by ships and a railroad across the isthmus. Aspinwall, who had been a frequent dinner guest at the Benton home, directed the captain of Jessie's ship to make her as comfortable as possible and arranged to have men from the railroad survey help her across the isthmus.

Jessie's father had planned to accompany her, but at the last minute he decided not to leave his invalid wife and sent Sarah's new husband, Richard Jacobs, instead. In addition Jessie was taking one of her favorite maids, a young free black woman named Harriet, who had grown up in the Benton household.

It was early in 1849 when Richard and Jessie, little Lily, the senator, and Harriet went to New York and took rooms at the Astor House while they waited for their ship. The city was jampacked, for news of gold in California had recently come, and thousands of men wanted to go west.

One day a crowd gathered in the hotel lobby, demanding to see Jessie, so she hurried down and found the lower halls filled by "a whole force of people." Jessie was defying the laws of New York, they said, by taking Harriet, "a free colored girl," out of the country against her will. This wasn't true, because Harriet was eager to go, but she was engaged to a young man who didn't want her to leave, and so had rounded up the protest.

Harriet, in tears, asked Jessie what she should do. The temper of the times was high. *Uncle Tom's Cabin*, a powerful book about slavery, had swept the country, and the movement for abolition was growing. Besides, Jessie knew how it felt to be in love. Therefore she advised the girl to stay behind and gave her a red silk dress to wear at her wedding.

"So I was not only to be without my father's care, but I had lost my last fragment of home," she later wrote. "There comes a dull edge to sorrow, which makes one accept new griefs without feeling." Jessie was genuinely fond of Harriet and would miss her. However, she and her father promptly engaged another maid, a middle-aged white woman from New England.

When at last they went to the ship, Jessie found she had been assigned two tiny staterooms, one for sleeping, one as a parlor, and Aspinwall had had them filled with flowers, fruit and books. Never having sailed before, Jessie didn't realize how roomy her quarters were, for a ship. She only knew that she was leaving her family, her friends, and everything she had ever known. It didn't help when she heard her father say, as he turned away after kissing her goodbye, "It is like leaving her in her grave."

Neither did it help when, the very first day at sea, her new maid turned out to be a thief, and the captain had to have her locked up. For the first time in her twenty-four years, Jessie was without a servant to help with the small problems of daily life.

Still, she had her brother-in-law Richard to keep her company, and her beloved little Lily to play with. She soon felt at home in her quarters and especially enjoyed the deck, where she could lie in the sun, or walk. Speaking of the power and majesty of the sea, she said, "I loved it at the first look."

At the tropical port of Chagres, on the Isthmus of Panama, where they had to leave the ship, the captain and Richard both tried to persuade her to return. Although someday a railroad would be built, they said, so far it was only begun. If she continued, she would have to climb aboard boats without gangplanks. Food would rot. Traveler after traveler had died.

"I thank you both," Jessie calmly said. "But I'm going on."

As the steamer rolled, Lily clutched a sturdy sailor tightly around his neck while he carried her down a bobbing ladder to the mail boat, "as small as a craft could be and still hold an engine," which was to take them eight miles up the Chagres River. With a determined clutch at her trailing skirts, Jessie followed, although it seemed like stepping down upon a toy. Nearing the shore, where she smelled stale fish, tar, cinnamon, refuse, human sweat, she was sure she would be ill, but fought it down.

Compared to what followed, even this tiny boat was a luxury, for eight miles upriver passengers were to transfer to pongos—dugout canoes poled by naked natives. These narrow craft rocked so crazily, low in the water, that at sight of them even placid little Lily clung in terror to her mother's hand.

However, Jessie was met by a Mr. Tucker from the railroad company, who gave her and her family space in the company pongo. "You'll be the only woman aboard," he said, "but you'll be safe. This crew has often carried my own wife to our headquarters."

Now for three days Jessie, Richard and Lily were poled up the slow, brown, jungle stream, its banks so covered with tangles of white and scarlet bloom that they glided along an aisle of flowers. At night they

Travel on the Chagres River, with passengers seated in the rear of each pongo. (From Mountains and Molehills, *by Frank Marryat, 1855.)*

camped in clean company tents on shore, with canvas floors and great fires that burned all through the hours of darkness, while strange animals hooted and howled nearby.

Just before reaching headquarters at Gorgona, thirty miles upstream, the boat grounded, and Richard jumped into the water to help drag it free. But suddenly "his eyes rolled back in his head" as he fell prostrate with a sunstroke. For a whole night the company doctor doubted that he would live, and when he revived, it was clear he could not go on.

"Return with me," he begged Jessie, but as before she refused. Reluctantly he then started back down the river, leaving her and Lily in care of the kindly men of the railroad company.

When they reached Gorgona, they had a brief rest. The *alcalde*, the mayor, invited her to a meal in his house, intending it to be an honor. Instead it was an ordeal, for the main dish was "baked monkey, which looked like a little child burned to death." Fighting down her horror, Jessie managed to eat a few bites.

Then it was time to begin the twenty-one-mile muleback ride over the isthmus—a "distance, not a road." Mule caravans had crossed here for centuries, and water had worn the rocks until the path went through a ditch that was at times twelve feet deep. Other parts were "a mule staircase," with occasional steps four feet high. Since there were no bridges across the narrow streams, Jessie had to cling tightly while her animal gathered his feet together and jumped. Sturdy little pig-tailed Lily laughed to see them crowded into the narrow trough, and thought it a special joke when one rubbed off its load on a convenient rock, but Jessie later said, "The whole thing was so like a nightmare that we took it as a bad dream—in helpless silence." After two grueling days, the group reached a point from which they looked down on the Pacific Ocean, and then they wound down into the walled city of Panama.

It was ancient, all stucco and tile, with jutting balconies that overhung the narrow streets. Although Jessie

Crossing the Isthmus of Panama by muleback. This is a humorous picture, but such conditions actually existed. (From Mountains and Molehills, *by Frank Marryat, 1855.)*

had expected to sail immediately on the ship *California*, this was impossible because it was lying abandoned in San Francisco Bay, its crew gone to the gold mines. She was stranded, along with thousands of others. But when she showed her letter of introduction to Madame Arcé y Zimena, aunt of the minister from New Granada, Madame Arcé took her into her own home.

This was "a great barracks of a house with ceilings twenty feet high and barn doors for windows." Except for her impatience to go on, Jessie was happy there, for it was clean and cool. She walked on the crumbling city walls at sunset; she and her hostess called on numerous Arcé relatives; and nuns from the nearby convent brought her *dulces*, a candy made from fresh fruit and sugar.

When newspapers were finally brought across the isthmus, they carried stories about her husband. Crossing the Rockies in blizzards had brought unimaginable hardships, the stories said. It was unlikely that Frémont had survived this, the worst winter on record. He must be dead by now. Even so, she refused to give up hope.

Eventually she received a long letter from Frémont himself, describing his disastrous trip, on which guides had been treacherous, and ten men had died of starvation. But he himself was now safe in the New Mexico home of Kit Carson, and he was well except for a frozen leg which might have to be amputated.

The ending was hopeful. "We shall yet, dearest wife, enjoy quiet and happiness together. I make pictures of the happy home we are to have, and oftenest

*Christmas with Frémont on his fourth expedition, in
the deep snow that nearly cost him his life. (From*
Life and Public Service of John Charles Frémont, *by
John Bigelow, 1856.)*

and among the pleasantest of all I see our library with
its bright fire in the rainy, stormy days, and the large
windows looking out upon the sea."

By now the rainy season of Panama was bringing torrents that pounded on the tiled roof and sent rivulets trickling down the inner walls. All day, every day, Jessie heard the splash and gurgle of water. It was cold. She fell seriously ill, being at times delirious, and having several hemorrhages of the lungs, which often signaled the dread consumption. However, with tender care from the Arcé family she survived and began to regain strength.

Late one night, when Jessie had been in Panama for seven weeks, she heard a loud boom, and the streets were filled with an uproarious crowd, rushing wildly about, singing, shouting, dancing in the moonlight. In a few minutes came another boom—and bedlam.

"We're off to California!" the dancers shouted. "Get ready! Get aboard!"

Moments later Madame Arcé rushed down the hall to say that not one, but two steamers had arrived, the *Panama* from around the horn, and the *California* from San Francisco with a shanghaied crew—men who had been seized and forced to sail the ship. Almost at once the captain of the *Panama* came in, looking for Jessie. He was going back to New York, and he was certain the colonel couldn't possibly meet her. She should go with him, he pleaded, rather than arrive alone in San Francisco, which was frantic with the rush for gold.

Jessie smiled—and refused. Saying a hasty goodbye to Madame Arcé, she hurried to the waterfront, boosted Lily into a tub at the end of a stout pole, climbed in after her, and was hoisted onto the ship.

It was packed, for it had quarters for only eighty, but four hundred were taking passage, and the whole deck was covered with sleeping men. Being a woman, Jessie was given a stateroom, but it was so hot she couldn't sleep in it. Therefore the sailors made her a tent on deck by throwing a large flag across the spanker boom. There she and Lily and another passenger, a Mrs. Gray, rested as best they could while the ship plunged ahead through the tropical night, with creaking timbers and the splash of waves.

She knew that Mr. Frémont might not have survived the trip, that he might have turned back east, that his leg might have been taken off. But she was near her goal now. If he had come to California, no matter what his condition, she was going to find him.

T E N

Jessie and the Gold Rush

1849

SHELTERED BY THE FLAG, surrounded by jubilant passengers, full of hope, Jessie was at first delighted with life aboard ship. She spent daytime hours walking in the sunshine and slept peacefully in the warm tropical nights.

But when they ran through a heavy rain storm, she fled to her stateroom, along with Lily and Mrs. Gray, who had shared her flag-tent. Even so, she caught a severe cold and began again to cough up blood.

Three weeks from Panama, when they reached the harbor of San Diego, she locked herself in her cabin, for she wanted to be alone in case she received bad news from Mr. Frémont. Suddenly she heard her fellow passengers knocking on her door and shouting that messages had come from shore.

"The colonel's safe!"

"He's gone to meet you at San Francisco."

"He didn't lose his leg. It was only frostbitten."

Mr. Frémont was alive.

The *Panama* continued up the coast until June 4, when its gun boomed as they moved into San Francisco Bay. Here deserted vessels swung with the tide, and row upon row of shacks and tents littered the treeless hills, half-veiled by fog. It was cold.

Since wharves hadn't yet been built, passengers carried Jessie and Lily and Mrs. Gray ashore through the surf. Shouting, bearded men were milling about beside the pier, but search as she would, Jessie couldn't find her husband. The waiting wasn't over, after all.

Shipboard friends then had her taken to Parker House, on the central plaza, where she was put to bed in a drab little drafty room. Since doctors weren't available, the faithful Mrs. Gray looked after her for ten weary days—noisy days and noisier nights, for most of the Parker House was occupied by gamblers. Auctioneers chanted, hammers pounded, music blared from saloons.

At last Jessie heard a man call out, "Your wife's inside the house, Colonel," and almost at once Mr. Frémont burst through the door, half smothering her in his arms. "You have been ill; you are ill now, my darling," he murmured.

Just then the door flew open and Lily came in, a solemn, rather fat child, with her hair in pigtails. Rising, the colonel gave her a fatherly hug and sat down with her on his lap.

"You didn't come," the little girl said. "Mother almost died. A lady downstairs says she will die."

San Francisco streets in the winter of 1849 were a sea
of mud, crossed by using boxes, planks and any kind of
trash as stepping stones. (From Mountains and ....
Molehills, by Frank Marryat, 1855.)

"She is partly right," Jessie agreed. "Being away
from you is a kind of death. Only with you am I fully
alive and well."

When they were a little more calm, Frémont told
her that on his way from Kit Carson's home to California, he had passed a caravan of twelve hundred men,
women and children, shouting and singing. They said
they were headed for fortune—the gold fields near Sacramento. Since he had left the East before news of gold
arrived, this was astonishing news, and he was still
more astonished to realize that his own ranch, the Mari-

posas (meaning butterflies) was near the mines. So he had hired twenty-five Mexicans who were already at work, digging for gold on shares.

Gold! thought Jessie. Would they truly be rich? Eagerly she began planning to go to the Mariposas with him.

However, she continued to cough up blood, so Mr. Frémont insisted that she must not live in a rough mining camp, nor in foggy San Francisco. Instead they moved south to the village of Monterey, where it was warm and sunny. She was to stay there, while he ran the mines and came to see her whenever he could.

Here, in what was then the capital of California, the only place for rent was part of a long, low, tile-roofed adobe, built around a courtyard. Nevertheless, Jessie was home at last—home being two unfurnished rooms, with the rolling sea on one side and a primitive, Spanish-speaking village on the other.

Her life was one long bewilderment. She wasn't strong, she was generally alone, and she had little money. In addition, shopping was a nuisance, for coins were so scarce that raw gold was used instead. Every store had miniature scales for weighing the precious dust, which shoppers carried in little leather bags.

Jessie knew nothing about housework or cooking, and finding food was difficult.

"Every eatable thing had been eaten off the face of the country," she later wrote. "I suppose there was not a fowl left, consequently not an egg. There were no cows, consequently no milk. Housekeeping deprived of

The harbor and village of Monterey, Jessie's first real home in California. This picture was made in 1846, three years before her arrival. (From A Tour of Duty in California, *by J. W. Revere, 1849.)*

milk, eggs, vegetables, and fresh meat, becomes a puzzle."

She made endless experiments, trying to figure out menus and recipes. "I could write a cookery book on 'How to Do Without,'" she said. "Rice is a great reliance when you learn its many uses."

Since they needed furniture, Frémont went to San Francisco and bought what Jessie considered "a prodigal amount" of whatever he could find—French damask, bamboo couches, heavily carved chairs. He also bought tin candlesticks, and—since he couldn't find any wash-basins—two English china punch bowls instead. The effect was somewhat startling, for Jessie now had Chinese brocade curtains, white-washed adobe walls, a large bronze Buddha—and a grizzly bearskin on the floor. She called it "true to the period, Pioneer Forty-Nine."

Household help was lacking, everything must be done by hand, and Jessie was frail. At first they relied on a free black named Saunders Jacobs, who had come West with Frémont to be their cook. But Saunders learned that if he could pay $1,700, he could free his wife and children, who were still slaves. Although he couldn't save this much as a cook, he could earn it quickly in the mines. Therefore, with Jessie's willing consent, Frémont gave him a job at the Mariposas.

The only other servants Jessie could hire were two young Indians named Juan and Gregorio, who had been on some of Frémont's expeditions. Even though they were kind, loyal and eager to help, their idea of a good meal was a stew cooked in an iron kettle over an open fire and so spicy it brought tears to the eyes.

One day a Texan came to the door with a strong young black girl whom he wanted to sell. If Jessie could have hired her for wages, she would have been overjoyed, but she firmly refused to buy a human being, even if she'd had the money. She would rather make do with Gregorio and his concoctions.

At last a woman named Mrs. McEvoy came, carrying a big, healthy baby. "Do you want a servant, Madam?" she asked.

"The worst in the world."

"I went to the general's," the woman said, referring to the commanding officers of the Monterey garrison. "He would have engaged me, but when I said I was from Australia, that I had come on the ship that just landed, he would hear nothing more. There *had* been a mutiny on board, but we were honest passengers, and I have all my references."

"Your baby is reference enough," Jessie told her. "He is so clean and fat and fond of you."

The search was over.

With Mrs. McEvoy in charge, Jessie began to regain health, and by late summer Mr. Frémont decided she was well enough to go to San Francisco with him. This became a long, joyous camping trip.

Before leaving the East, he had ordered a six-seated surrey, which had finally come around the horn. It was a remarkable vehicle, tall and large, with red leather seats, which could be made into a bed. It was pulled by two mules, a big, white, slow patient one named Job, and a brisk little brown fellow named Picayune, meaning tiny. This became Jessie's temporary home.

Leaving Mrs. McEvoy to care for the house, they started off through sun-warmed hills. First, on a spirited horse, came Frémont, making sure of the way and occasionally galloping back to check on Jessie. Next, the high, swaying carriage drawn by Job and Picayune and driven by a young Lieutenant Beale, a close friend. Jessie rode on one of its red leather seats—pale, smiling, wrapped in her husband's blue army cape—with red-cheeked Lily facing her. And at the rear trudged Juan and Gregorio, wearing broad red sashes, red scarves around their heads under stiff sombreros, and leading two pack mules.

It was warm, and Jessie was enchanted with the blue skies and soft breeze. They passed yellowing wild oats, groves of trees, herds of grazing cattle. Finding no roads, they followed half-hidden horse trails, and when these were steep or rough, the Indians put ropes around the carriage to steady it.

At twilight, while Gregorio made one of his blistering stews, Jessie walked peacefully around camp enveloped in the army cape. When she offered to help, Mr. Frémont told her she had only one job—to rest and get well. After supper they sat by a campfire singing and telling stories until bedtime, when the men turned the carriage seats to make Jessie's bed. Lily slept in the "boot"—the bulging end of the carriage—and the men outside. By nine o'clock all was still except the crackle of the fire and steady munching of the mules.

Day followed day as they pushed on north. At the village of San Jose they hired some Indian women to wash their clothes by putting them in a brook and pounding them between stones. Here they were met by a workman from the Mariposas, bringing buckskin bags filled with gold dust and nuggets—the first treasure from their mines. Since there were no banks, they put the bags under a straw mattress for safety that night, then sent them to Monterey, to be kept in trunks in their rooms.

*San Francisco in 1849, when Jessie arrived there, was a
straggling city of tents and shacks. This drawing shows
some of the ships that had been abandoned when their
crews went to the gold mines.* (From A Yankee Trader
in the Gold Rush, *by Franklin A. Buck. Courtesy of the
Bancroft Library.)*

Next they stopped in San Francisco, where Frémont had business. Here, because the hotels were so
rough, he bought Jessie a tiny, Chinese-built house,
which fitted together like a puzzle, its walls and floor,
doors and windows, sliding in grooves. The only nails
in the whole structure were those in the shingles, and
it was just big enough for a bed. The men erected this
miniature house on some low sand dunes just outside
the city, where Jessie slept in it, with Mr. Frémont in
the carriage and the Indians camping nearby.

They stayed for ten days. Once Saunders rode in
with another rich convoy of gold. He remained as cook,

JESSIE'S JOURNEY TO CALIFORNIA
AND HER HOMES IN THE WEST~1848

1. New York City   3. Monterey   5. Las Mariposas
2. San Diego   4. San Francisco   6. San Jose

☐ States   ☐ Territories   ☐ Acquired in
                                        Mexican War

and Frémont's business friends often rode out from the city to share a picnic feast, with bundles of leftover shingles for tables and chairs. Many of these guests were educated men with a broad view of the world, a delight for Jessie, who loved good conversation. Overhead was the blue sky, underfoot the dunes spangled with blue lupine. She never forgot those picnic meals on the sun-warmed sand overlooking the bay.

But now it was autumn—time for the rains, for the cold winds, time to take shelter. And the adobe home in Monterey promised a brand new excitement.

By this time Mexico had yielded California to the United States, but Congress had not yet made it into either a state or a territory. Instead, it was still under army control, its head being Governor General Bennet Riley, at the Monterey army barracks. He, however, had no authority to set up civil laws, courts, or jails, or to make decisions about the old Mexican land titles. This was serious, because most gold miners were trespassers, digging where they wished, without control.

Early that summer General Riley had decided that since Congress wouldn't act, Californians must take things into their own hands, and he had called delegates to a convention that would establish either a state or a territory. This convention was about to meet in Monterey.

So Jessie eagerly helped Frémont pack their gear, told Saunders goodbye, and started south. She was headed for the scene of action.

Politics and Gold

1849-1850

IN SEPTEMBER, when Jessie's marvelous carriage rolled into Monterey, she found the delegates already assembling. Some were business men, some were bearded miners, others were ranchers who rode in on horseback with serapes over their shoulders.

Jessie was absolutely enchanted to be near politics again. "I can smell Washington air," she said, and invited delegates to her home. Aided by Mrs. McEvoy, she enlarged the dining table with planks, and served ample meals, her best dessert being a spicy pudding from a recipe which she herself had invented—using rice.

Since very few American women lived in the area, the men considered these visits a rare treat. They delighted Jessie, too, for she thought conversation far more important than food. Eagerly she joined the arguments around her fireside, arguments for which she was armed through clippings and newspapers sent by her father.

The men soon realized how well-informed she was. "If you want the real Washington situation with well-thought-out opinions on it, ask Miss Jessie," one of them said.

The biggest issue was slavery. Some thought California should allow slaves, others wanted it free, while still others thought it should be divided into two states, free in the North, slave in the South. Having spent so much time at Cherry Grove, Jessie knew how much ease slavery could bring, but she wanted none of it.

"You will be the richest woman in the world if your mines are worked by slave labor," a proslavery delegate urged.

"Surely we should keep the spirit of liberty in this land which now breathes that spirit," she insisted.

"Fine sentiment, Mrs. Frémont. But the aristocracy will always have slaves."

"Why not an aristocracy of emancipators?" she replied. "We Bentons freed our slaves long ago." She reminded them that she had done her own housework rather than own a slave-girl, and that she had gladly sent Saunders to the mines so he could free his family.

"It isn't a pretty sight for a child to see and hear chain gangs clanking through the streets, or to watch officers chasing a fugitive slave and putting him in irons," she said, remembering her childhood. "Never will I consent to own or use a slave."

Knowing how she felt, one delegate brought fifteen others to hear it from her own lips. When she finished speaking, a tall, rough-looking man burst out, "All the

*Slaves being marched in chains through Washington,
D.C. Jessie never forgot scenes such as this, which were
common when she was a child. (Courtesy of the
Library of Congress.)*

women here are crying to have servants—but if you, a
Virginia lady, can get along without, they shan't have
them—we'll keep clear of slave labor."

They were listening to her! Jessie thought. She felt
it "a true happiness" to help keep the California won-
derland free.

Day after day, the delegates met in nearby Colton Hall, and day after day Jessie was in the audience, listening as they put together a state constitution. In the end, to her satisfaction, they banned slavery.

When it was finished and the last signature in place, she joined the street crowd while the flag was unfurled and harbor guns fired once for every state in the union. At the thirty-first shot the village rocked with the shout, "That's for California."

Laughing and crying for joy, Jessie then rushed to her two rooms to dress for the dance. Her "ball gown"— a coarse red blouse and navy-blue skirt made by cutting off the tail of her riding habit—was no worse than others. One smallish delegate spent an uncomfortable evening in pinned-up pantaloons lent by an officer who weighed two hundred pounds.

The next steps were to elect officials and have the new constitution approved by the United States Congress. Since by now Mr. Frémont's mines had made him wealthy, and since he was also famous, he was asked to run for the national Senate—a dazzling prospect, to Jessie. If she could go to Washington as wife of a senator, that would be sweet indeed, after the shame of the court-martial.

But as the winter rains continued, she was lonely, for her husband was generally gone and the new legislature was meeting at San Jose, which had been chosen as capital. Jessie's little fling at politics was over. Housebound, she listened to the rain and wondered whether her husband could indeed be elected.

*Frémont in 1850, just after they
moved to California. Of all his
pictures, this is the one the family
liked best. (Courtesy of the Bancroft
Library.)*

While she waited, she spent much time in sewing,
for her clothes and Lily's were nearly worn out. She
bought whatever material she could find, carefully
ripped up their one set of underclothes to make patterns,
and sewed new pantalets and petticoats—all by hand.
She tried to copy her one black silk dress, but she had

lost so much weight that it hung in bunches.

One day Mr. Frémont came down in a blinding rainstorm to show her pieces of gold quartz from a vein that was two feet thick at the surface and wider below. His early mines had really been "diggings," near the surface and easy to reach. But this quartz would mean burrowing into the earth and crushing tons of rock, an expensive operation—and a fortune.

Even wealth couldn't buy luxury. Once, when a friend congratulated Jessie, she replied, "Gold isn't much as an end, is it? It can't conjure comforts nor an ounce of brain rations. I'm simply famishing for the taste of a good book." All she had were five bound volumes of the *London Times*, some poetry of Byron, a collection of *Merchant's Magazines*, and *The Arabian Nights*.

On the dark afternoon of December 22, she lighted candles and sat beside the fire, showing Lily pictures. Mrs. McEvoy was nearby, sewing, while the McEvoy baby played on the bearskin rug. Suddenly horse's feet clattered along the road and stopped, and the door opened, letting in a shower of raindrops. When Jessie looked up, she saw her husband leaning against the doorsill, dripping all over the tiled floor, and laughing.

"I can only stay the night!" he exclaimed. "I must go back early in the morning." He had ridden the seventy-five miles from San Jose to tell her he had won the election. They were to sail at New Year's, just ten days off.

For that joyous Christmas Jessie decorated a tree

with balls of tinfoil and stars cut from sardine cans. While her husband arranged to leave his mines in the care of agents, she packed their belongings—pitifully few, for a wealthy senator and his family. Saunders, who had earned enough to free his family, was going with them, but Juan and Gregorio and Mrs. McEvoy were to stay behind.

On New Year's night when the ship's gun went off, rain was falling in torrents and the streets were running brooks. Gregorio carried Lily to the wharf, while Frémont carried Jessie, and Saunders supervised their luggage. They all climbed into a large rowboat, which another Indian rowed out to the ship. There the loyal Gregorio wept so bitterly that Jessie said his tears fairly waterlogged their boat.

And then they were watching through gray rain as they passed through the Golden Gate. In their joy they laughed and quoted a favorite song.

> *What care I for wind or rain*
> *When I'm coming back again.*

The new senator and his lady were on their way.

TWELVE

The Senator's Lady

1850-1851

ALTHOUGH AT FIRST Jessie, Mr. Frémont and Lily all felt well, by the time they reached Panama, Jessie was ill with one of the dread tropical fevers. A friend who saw her there remarked, "Pioneering is hell on women. That child is all eyes and grit. Nothing else left."

In spite of her condition, they somehow had to cross the dreadful isthmus, so they had a sailor's hammock swung between two poles, with a sunshade above it. The Indians carried it smoothly, two at a time, Madame Arcé provided a crimson pillow trimmed with lace, and the party set out. As Jessie was being carried through town in her swaying hammock, she overheard a bystander comment in Spanish, "Oh! The poor thing! What a pity to die so far from her country!"

She was faintly aware of the trip, up the mule trail, down the other side to the Chagres River, and then in a dugout canoe. At the Atlantic port of Chagres she was lashed in a chair and hoisted over the ship's side, then tied with sheets to a sofa. Later on, a doctor told her, "By all the rules, you should have died."

Two days after sailing, Jessie's head cleared, but by then Lily and Mr. Frémont both had the fever, with Saunders caring for them all. Frémont was raving in delirium about green hillsides and cold spring water; Lily's head had been shaved—a common treatment for fever—and she was babbling.

"Go lie down!" she said. "There's a big storm—the captain comes in and he's funny, like Santa Claus, with icicles on his beard—and never mind my hair—it's cooler without braids—only please go lie down."

The three Frémonts lay in their bunks, rolling and tossing, while the ship plowed north through stormy winter seas. But they were young, and clung to life. Three months later when the ship steamed into New York harbor, it was spring and they were on their feet again.

In the hotel, when Jessie glanced at a long mirror, she was shocked to see herself—only twenty-five years old, but sunken-eyed, skin yellow from fever, dressed in a brown, ill-fitting blouse, shapeless navy-blue skirt, and a large, outdated hat tied on with a bedraggled scarf. Beside her stood fat, red-cheeked Lily, almost bursting out of a too-small brown dress, with coarse muslin pantalets and buckskin shoes. Her shaven head was wrapped in a black silk handkerchief, because her only hat had blown overboard. So this was the senator's wife

A mother and daughter, from an article about fashions in dress. Jessie and Lily must have bought clothing much like this when they came to Washington from California. (From Harper's New Monthly Magazine, *June, 1856.)*

from California! thought Jessie. Without wasting a moment, she took herself and Lily to a dressmaker and ordered smart new wardrobes.

When at last they reached the Benton home in Washington, she could hardly contain her joy. "I took sedate little walks down Pennsylvania Avenue, in the spring twilight," she wrote, "but I wanted to run and shout, to hug the tree trunks, to drop down on the ground and lay my cheek against the new grass, to kiss the crocuses and wild violets, and to float away upon that misty gray-green cloud of young leaves above me."

Washington was fairyland. As the senator's lady, Jessie made a joyous round of teas and dinner parties. She had long, refreshing talks with her father and his friends about books and politics, blowing away "the cobwebs and mold" of her days in the West. She spent happy hours with Madame Bodisco, her old friend Harriet, who had been the rejected May Queen and was now a wealthy widow.

"This was our year of compensations," she wrote. "It seemed as though the storms of fate made this last outburst only to disappear and leave unclouded the wonderful joy of the return."

But some congressmen weren't willing to admit California, because its new constitution made it a free state and upset the balance between North and South. It was fall by the time they reached a compromise that provided for a stricter return of runaway slaves (to please the South) and the admission of California as a free state (to please the North). On September 19, 1850,

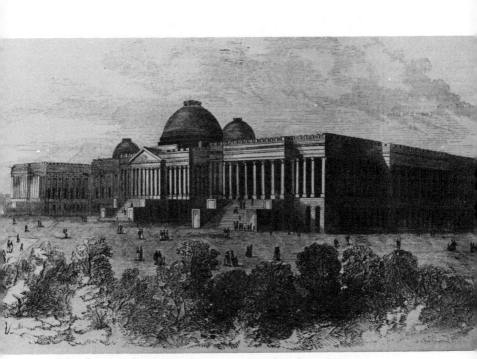

The Capitol building in 1852, shortly after the new wings were added. This was the year Jessie came to Washington as a senator's wife. (From Gleason's Pictorial Drawing Room Companion, *Volume 2, 1852.)*

Jessie sat proudly in the gallery while Mr. Frémont and the other California senator, William M. Gwin, took their seats.

She had only a short time to enjoy it. One senator was to have a long term, with the other serving only until March 3, and as was the custom, the terms were decided by lot. Although in California Frémont had received more votes than Gwin, he drew the short one. After her perilous trip and nearly losing her life, Jessie must now pack up and do it all over again. But ever since she was a child she had spent weeks of every year traveling, and if she felt dismayed, she didn't show it.

She and Mr. Frémont talked it over. He was so popular, they were sure he could easily run again, and this time win a full term of office. It was a bother, nothing more. Because she was pregnant, he wanted her to stay in Washington while he made the journey alone, but she would hear nothing of that. They'd already been separated much too often.

"I've thought it all out," she said. "Reliable stretcher bearers with a chair instead of a cot for the land trip, proper foods which we take along, tea equipment, and plenty of quinine. And awaiting us there will be the faithful Gregorio."

Just as she planned, the journey went so smoothly that after being away for a little more than a year, they were safely back in California. Since Jessie was well now, they rented a furnished house high on a hill overlooking San Francisco and the bay with its bustle of shipping. She wanted to rehire Mrs. McEvoy, but that good friend and helper was now living with her own husband, so Gregorio took full charge of the kitchen. He was blissfully happy to be with them, but resentful because instead of a campfire or fireplace, he had to cook on a stove, which he called the "black iron box."

"*Caramba!*" (The devil!) he would exclaim with a vicious bang of its door.

Frémont spent as much time as possible in San Jose, where the state legislature was meeting and would decide the new election. However, during the past months many southerners had moved in, making the proslavery forces so strong that vote after vote was taken without a majority for anyone. By the one hundred forty-second ballot it was still not settled—and Frémont wanted to develop the quartz veins at the Mariposas. This meant he must buy machinery, erect buildings, and hire help. In addition, his title was based on a Mexican land grant which had never been clear and should be straightened out. With little time for campaigning, he lost the election.

Jessie had had a taste of glory as a senator's lady, but that was over now. She was an ordinary citizen again.

THIRTEEN

"Our Jessie"

1851-1856

FOR JESSIE, the next few years were a dizzying roller coaster of ups and downs. On April 19, 1851, three months after her return to California, she gave birth to a son whom she named John Charles and considered, "the healthiest, most living and lovable baby boy imaginable."

Fifteen days later she heard fire bells and screams. Looking out, she saw smoke, for a paint shop was on fire in the center of town. San Francisco was a city of wood, with planked streets and shingled roofs; fanned by strong sea breezes, block after block was burned. Jessie's home was spared that day, but two months later, when fire bells clanged again, she watched its total destruction. However, friends saved most of the furnishings, and with Gregorio's help they were soon reestablished.

Jessie had been through so much—the hard trip west, the birth of little Charley, and two fires—that she

The San Francisco Fire of 1851, which destroyed Jessie's home while she watched from a hill. (From A Yankee Trader in the Gold Rush *by Franklin A. Buck. Courtesy of the Bancroft Library.)*

began to have blinding headaches. She slept poorly, often waking with the memory of fire bells, and rushing to open a window. Mr. Frémont decided she must get away for a rest and change.

One evening in December as she was making sardine-can stars for another makeshift Christmas, he abruptly asked, "How would you like a trip to Paris as a New Year's gift?"

"Splendid!" she replied. "Let's also give Charley a closer peep at the man in the moon."

Smiling, he handed her a packet of steamer tickets. It was all arranged.

This meant another journey across the isthmus, with Charley tied by a tablecloth to the back of an Indian, and then by ship across the Atlantic for a glorious year in the capitals of Europe.

Twenty-seven years old, slender, with pink and white complexion and alert hazel-brown eyes, Jessie was still a beauty, and her husband was famous. In England, wearing a pink gown trimmed with roses, she was presented to Queen Victoria and entertained by aristocrats. In Paris she lived in an ornate house where her bath water flowed from the beaks of silver swans into a marble tub. The Frémonts attended balls and dinners, met royalty. Although they were invited to the Emperor Napoleon's wedding, they declined because Jessie was pregnant again.

But the ups and downs weren't over. First came word that Jessie's brother Randolph had suddenly died of malaria, and she was inconsolable. She kept to her room for weeks, weeping until she felt she would lose her sight.

Next came the birth of the new baby, a little daughter named Anne, after which they returned to Washington and rented a house near Jessie's parents. There, during an epidemic of digestive ailments, baby Anne died. This time, to everyone's surprise, Jessie was pale and still. As Frémont told some friends, "It was she who remained dry-eyed to comfort me, for I was unmanned."

Now the roller coaster picked up speed. In 1853, Frémont went on another privately-backed expedition (his fifth and last) to find an all-weather route for a railroad, while Jessie waited in Washington. This time he again crossed the mountains in winter, and again nearly lost his life, but came home safely at last. On May 17, 1854, soon after his return, Jessie gave birth to a healthy baby boy whom they named Frank Preston, for her favorite Virginia cousin. With three living children, she was a busy and happy young mother.

Next, in the following September, while her father was away, her mother lay down for a nap, and later on Jessie discovered that she was dead. This shock was made infinitely more cruel because the senator couldn't forgive himself for not having been there.

"After all my years of watching, she looked for me in vain," he bitterly said. "You had my place. I cannot bear it—forgive me, child, but I don't want to see you—not now."

So Jessie felt the double loss of mother and father.

Two more blows followed in quick succession. Benton had already been defeated as senator because Missouri was a slave state, and he opposed slavery. He had then been elected to the House of Representatives instead. Now he had to run again—and he lost.

Within a few weeks his house caught fire, and Jessie watched helplessly while it burned to the ground. The whole library of beautiful books was gone, along with the manuscript of his second volume of memoirs, which she had helped him write.

The old politician stood beside Jessie, watching the flames. "It all makes the less to leave, child," he said. "All is gone that made my life. This makes it easy to die."

For Jessie, the one bright spot was that after all these misfortunes, he became close to her again.

And now came the greatest rise and the greatest dip of all.

The issue of slavery was still threatening to split the nation. There were three parties: Democrats, including Benton, who were strongly Southern and proslavery; Whigs, once well established, but now divided on the question of slavery and losing strength; Know-Nothings, who were mostly interested in stopping immigration into the United States. There wasn't any antislavery political organization.

To fill this gap, a mass meeting had recently formed a new party called Republican, to fight the growth of slavery. So far this group was small, although it was growing fast, and in 1855, Frémont was asked to be its candidate for president.

By now the Frémonts were living in New York, and Jessie with the children had gone to Nantucket Island off the coast of Massachusetts to escape the summer heat. Changing his political party was such an important decision that Frémont went there to consult her.

He found her wearing a light blue gown with a ribbon around her hair, having tea on the terrace with the children. Thirteen-year-old Lily was holding the baby Frank, while Charley was leaning against his mother's knee and listening to a story. Jessie was thirty-one years old now, and still beautiful. Mr. Frémont was entranced at the picture.

That evening toward sunset they went for a long walk to Lighthouse Hill, where they sat on a bench high above the surf and talked. Many Democrats wanted Frémont to stay in their party and run for president—a tempting prospect which might place them in the White House. But it would mean endorsing slavery.

A second choice was to return to California and attend to the mines, the surest road to wealth.

Or they could become Republicans, which would drive a wedge between Jessie and her southern relatives. It was also the strongest stand they could take against slavery.

On and on they talked, as the sun went down and fog crept in, hiding the moon. "If you're unwilling," Frémont assured her, "I shall not accept."

Far below they could glimpse the dark remains of a ship embedded in the sand, while far above flashed the light, steady and brilliant. To Jessie these seemed symbols of her choice between "a wreck of dishonor, or the light of good." Much as she loved her cousins, hard as the choice would be, she felt that she and her husband must take a stand against a monstrous wrong.

Later she wrote, "There was only one decision possible, and when in the small hours we went in, the past lay behind me."

Mr. Frémont was going to try for the Republican nomination.

Only forty-three years old, slight but muscular, with lively blue eyes, curling beard and hair turning gray, he was a romantic figure. All winter, support for him grew and in June, the Republican convention nominated him on the first ballot. The band struck up a march, a Frémont flag was unfurled above the platform, and the crowd chanted, "Frémont! Frémont for President!" William L. Dayton of New York was nominated as vice-president, defeating a gangling lawyer named Abraham Lincoln.

For their candidate the Democrats chose James Buchanan, the same Buchanan who had stood with Jessie at the marriage of her school friend Harriet.

Soon the campaign was in full swing. Frémont headquarters were set up in downtown New York, and Jessie's house became a mail station and press clipping bureau. She offered meals to all comers eighteen hours a day. She answered personal and friendly letters, while other workers took care of business ones.

She was nearly as popular as her husband. Torchlight processions moved up Broadway to the curb before their house, and after Frémont made a speech from the steps, the crowd would shout, "Jessie Frémont! Jessie Benton!" until she appeared on the porch.

Song writers were busy. One popular song said,

> *And whom shall we toast for the Queen*
> *of the White House?*
> *We'll give them 'Our Jessie' again and again.*

A political cartoon of 1856, when Frémont was running for president. (From Jessie Benton Frémont, *by Catherine C. Phillips, 1935.)*

Wherever she went, she met young women in white with violets at their waists or wearing violet-colored muslins in honor of her favorite flower. Her hairdress, her manner of speech, were copied. Countless babies were named Jessie Anne. She sat up late answering letters, and a steady stream of callers demanded interviews upon religion, marriage, divorce, and politics.

Some tried to trip her. One terrifying woman in a bonnet shaped like a helmet abruptly said, "You're not as sensible-looking as the cartoons make you out." Consulting a little notebook, she then began to fire questions about Benton slaves in Washington, and about the girl Jessie had "tried to entice to California."

Jessie mildly assured her that the Washington servants were free, and that the black girl, also free, had stayed behind to be married in a new red silk dress, a gift from Jessie herself.

When tea was brought, the woman said, "I see you ape the English by serving tea and cake between meals."

"I find it a comforting break in my often wearying day," Jessie replied.

"But you serve it by a French maid."

"Yes." Jessie leaned forward like a conspirator and whispered, "But between us, I think I make better tea myself. I had no maid in Monterey. I heated the water in a long-handled iron saucepan over a smoky fire. Instead of French cakes, I lifted a sardine from his crowded can and gave him a decent burial between two soda crackers."

At this the tormentor laughed, and later on Jessie was happy to see a friendly report, which called her a good woman who could cook over a campfire.

Before long the campaign became bitter. News-

THERE IS THE WHITE HOUSE Y. IDER,

OR

THE FREMONT CAMPAIGN SONG

S. T. GORDON. 297. BROADWAY   NEW YORK
BOSTON OLIVER DITSON.   PHIL? J. E. GOULD.   CINCINNATI, D.A.TRUAX & BAY

The cover of a campaign song of 1856. The scenes in the corners refer to Frémont's adventures. (Courtesy of the Bancroft Library.)

papers trumpeted the fact that Frémont's parents weren't married until after his birth. He was ridiculed for his moustache and beard. Lies were spread—that he was a French actor, that Jessie had been suckled by a slave mammy, that she owned slaves now and watched them beaten.

"Do you want to see a Frenchman's bastard enter the White House, carrying a nigger-worshiper banner?" asked one attack.

All this wounded Mr. Frémont, who found it harder to face than wild beasts and blizzards, but Jessie was tough. The attacks that hurt her were from the warm southern family that she loved. They wrote bitter letters accusing her of treason to the South.

"This ended my old life," she said. "I was dropped by every relative." It was a lifelong sorrow.

Her father's blasts were even harder to bear, for he took to the lecture platform against them. Sincerely convinced that the nation was in danger of splitting and that the only way to prevent it was to move slowly on slavery, he called the Republicans "a motley mixture of malcontents with no real desire in any of them to save the Union."

"Do the people believe the South will submit to such a President as Frémont?" he roared. "We are treading on a volcano that is liable at any moment to break forth and overthrow the nation."

Even though the Republicans were growing in strength, they were a new party, and had a long way to go. By a month before election, both Frémont and Jessie had given up hope of winning. However, when results came in, they were surprisingly close. Of thirty-eight states, the Democrat, Buchanan, carried nineteen; Fillmore, the Whig, carried eight; and Frémont carried eleven. Most historians believe that if the Whigs hadn't split the antislavery vote, and if Jessie's father had supported her husband, the Frémonts would have moved into the White House.

Although Mr. Frémont and Jessie took the defeat calmly, the next morning at breakfast Lily laid her head on her arms and wept so violently that Jessie told her to dress for the street. While the child still sobbed, Jessie tied a thick green veil over her face, winding it around and around to hide the reddened eyes.

"Now go and walk," she said.

So Lily walked Washington Square, again and again, still weeping, until she recovered self-control. Calm at last, she returned to the house, where Jessie had a long talk with her on the need for courage.

The Frémont campaign wasn't a total loss, for he was strong, and his party was growing. Many hoped he would be elected another time, so that his own tact, plus Jessie's close ties with the South, might save the nation a war. Already there was talk of nominating him again at the next election.

All that was over now. Jessie carefully made a file of items from the campaign—cartoons, songs, letters and newspaper items—even the cruel ones. She was ready for private life. It would be an exciting life, she thought, for they were returning to California, and this time, rough as it was, Mr. Frémont was going to take her to the Mariposas.

FOURTEEN

Jessie and the Golden State

1856-1861

BY THE TIME Jessie reached the Mariposas it was spring, 1858, more than a year since the campaign. In the meantime she had paid a long, happy visit to her sister Susan in Paris, and had spent several months in Washington, near her father. She had been worried because he seemed ill, his towering form shrunken and his face pale. But he had insisted that she go with her husband.

"It isn't right for a family to be separated," he had said.

So here she was, after crossing the isthmus on the new railroad, sailing to San Francisco, and coming to these Sierra Nevada Mountains by horse.

The Mariposas was huge—44,306 acres, about seventy square miles. It included mountains and canyons, sagebrush and forest, ranches, a fine waterfall, and two primitive towns, Mariposa and Bear Valley. But the

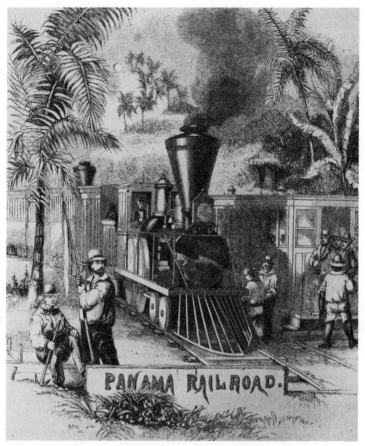

The Panama Railroad, completed in 1855, made Jessie's trips across the Isthmus of Panama much easier, safer and quicker. (From Harper's New Monthly Magazine, *January, 1859.)*

house they were to live in was only a shabby little adobe standing on a knoll half a mile from town, with a large, unpainted storehouse in back, and wild geraniums on the lawn. Butterflies were flitting among the flowers, birds were singing, and there was a steady thumping of stampmills and creak of ore-wagons—sounds of the mines.

Jessie sighed as she looked from the house to her family: Lily, age fifteen, sturdy, a bit stocky; the two little boys, Frank and Charley, ages seven and nearly four; Foxy—Douglass Fox, the son of friends, seventeen years old, tall and too thin and hoping to regain his health in the warm climate; and four servants. Somehow she had to figure out where all these people were to sleep and what they were to eat. She, wife of a wealthy gold miner, was to live like this!

First she must have the house enlarged, and as chief helper she enlisted a tenant named Biddle Boggs—tall, stooped, with a long face like wrinkled leather, and scanty yellow beard and hair.

"Me mother was a Biddle and me father a Boggs, and there you have it," he drawled, with a glint in his faded blue eyes.

Jessie had spotted several small log buildings nearby, which she asked Biddle Boggs to move, so he had them put on log rollers and drawn by oxen over the rough ground. Once in place, the buildings were connected with a long verandah—and there was room for everyone. When it was given a coat of whitewash, the villagers christened it "The White House."

Furnishing it was not difficult, for Bear Valley stores carried luxury items for wealthy miners. Jessie bought flowered French wallpaper, crimson velvet car-

*The town of Bear Valley, which was on Frémont's land.
Jessie spent her first night at the Mariposas in the Oso
House, a small hotel owned by her husband. (From*
Hutchings' California Magazine, *September, 1859.
Courtesy of the Bancroft Library.)*

pets, and rolls of silk draperies. She had purchased a
piano in San Francisco, and when it came by ox team,
she and the company blacksmith tuned it—she tapping
the key, he turning the peg until she cried, "Stop!"

One day while she was still busy with the house,
Frémont's lawyer and his wife rode out from town, and
Jessie went outside to meet them. Still in the saddle, the
lawyer's wife said, "I'm so glad to see you in colors and
cheerful again."

"Why not?" asked Jessie. "I am very well now."

"Oh—so soon after your father's death—" The rest was lost because her husband seized her bridle and led her away.

At once Frémont was at Jessie's side. "Is my father dead?" she asked. As tears filled her eyes, she faintly added, "When?"

For answer he took her in his arms, gently explaining that her father had died while they were still at sea, that word had recently come, and that he had been trying to gather courage to tell her. "I wish you need never have learned it," he whispered.

A few weeks later a letter from Eliza said that while they were still in Washington, Benton had known he was fatally ill with cancer of the stomach, but had refused to darken Jessie's visit by telling her. Instead, he had kept on his feet by the use of painkillers, and on the day she left, he had gone to bed, never to rise again.

It was a terrible blow, one from which Jessie was a long time recovering. However, she couldn't give way to sorrow, for she had a family to care for.

At first she could find little to eat but canned food. "It's like the fable of King Midas," she said. "Gold everywhere. Nothing but gold."

She solved it in part by giving waste water from the mines to a nearby Italian gardener who used it to irrigate his crops, then brought her fresh vegetables.

She made friends with everyone. Indian women flocked to listen while she gave their children lessons in the shade of a tree. "We were their matinee," she said.

She befriended miners' families. Much later a miner's son recalled her kindness, saying, "We children all loved 'Jessie.' "

To Lily, everything at the Mariposas was fun—she raised chickens, rode over the mountains, and visited the mills, where she liked to watch the pouring of liquid gold that glowed with colors like a driftwood fire. She had young Foxy for a friend.

But for Jessie it was exile. She rarely had a chance to talk about books or politics. Mail came only twice a month. She seldom rode, for deep down she was afraid of horses. And Mr. Frémont was often away, supervising the mines.

In summer, the heat became intolerable, with wind that blew like a furnace blast. When she wrote letters, Jessie had to lay several sheets of paper under her arm, for flesh couldn't stand the touch of hot marble. The young people made leather shoes for the dogs, to keep their feet from blistering. Every morning the animals would come to have their shoes put on, and in the evening would come again to have them taken off.

One hot night Jessie was awakened by a low voice saying, "Colonel, the Hornitos crowd have jumped the Black Drift."

"What does that mean?" she asked, in alarm.

"Only mining work," Mr. Frémont assured her. "It is cool now—go to sleep."

She did so, but when she awoke in the morning, he was gone.

Although the United States Congress had recently cleared Frémont's title, Chief Justice Terry of the California Supreme Court had ruled that any mine left unattended was free for anyone to take. As Jessie tartly put it, "By this was meant, if a man had gone to his breakfast, he was held to have given up his claim."

Some men without land had therefore organized a "league" called the Hornitos, with the aim of seizing mines.

Jessie's special protector, Isaac, part black and part Cherokee Indian, now told her what had happened. First, the Hornitos had bribed workers at Frémont's Black Drift mine to leave it. Next, the Hornitos had set up camp near the adjoining mine called Josephine. Under the law they couldn't take it because half a dozen men remained deep inside, so they were refusing to let anyone pass.

"Starve them out!" they cried, posting guards at every road. They were rough, ready to strike, wearing untidy beards, red shirts, overalls stuffed into high-topped boots, revolvers and bowie knives hanging to their belts—a dangerous lot.

Huddled in the White House, Jessie knew that somehow word had to be sent to the Governor at Sacramento. Although she refused to let Lily ride for help on her favorite horse, Ayah, she decided that young Foxy could try it. Together he and Lily muffled Ayah's hooves with rags, Isaac told Foxy where to find a friendly camp, and then the young man started up a dry creek bed, hidden by manzanita and chapparal. Fearfully

Jessie peered through the dust as the slim figure moved away and vanished.

The next afternoon a messenger rode to the White House door and handed her a note which threatened to burn the house and kill the colonel unless she left within twenty-four hours.

"No answer," Jessie crisply told the rider. She didn't feel as brave as she sounded, but she was sure that—under the unjust new law—leaving her house now would risk losing it forever.

While she was still wondering what to do, Foxy rode in, "fair and calm, with the light of victory in his eyes." He had found the campers, who would send word to the governor.

This was just the news Jessie needed. "Hitch the carriage horses to the best wagon, with the blue rosettes in their harness," she told Isaac. "And you dress up, too."

Putting on a French dress of white muslin, with lilac ribbons and a little purple velvet bonnet, she picked up a white parasol and climbed into the wagon. "Drive to Bates Tavern," she said, for that was league headquarters, and its owner was a friend of the ringleaders.

Once there, she sent for Mr. Bates. "What they demand is against the law." She spoke in an icy tone, sitting very straight under the parasol. "You may come and kill us—we are but women and children, and it will be easy—*but you cannot kill the law.*"

A rather meek, timid man, Mr. Bates listened quietly, overawed because Jessie was so angry.

"If the house is burned," she continued, "we will camp on the land. If the men kill the colonel, we will sell the property to a corporation which will be much harder to deal with than he is." She told him about Foxy's ride.

With a final shake of her parasol she then commanded Isaac, "You can drive home now." While the wagon turned, she held her head high, although cold quivers were running down her back and she expected a shot at any moment. When at last she was safe at home, she sank into a chair and burst into sobs.

That night, with Isaac and Biddle Boggs on guard, she and Lily were awakened by bombs made of tin cans. But no one harmed the house, and in a few days the Hornitos siege was broken.

Still later, when all was quiet again, a committee of miners' wives put on their finest, ruffled dresses and came on horseback to tell her how grateful they were.

"If you had gone away," they said, "the men would have begun fighting, and these hills would have run blood." Most of the neighbors agreed that Jessie's courage had prevented a catastrophe.

Through the snows of winter she stayed at the Mariposas, but the next summer Mr. Frémont took her to San Francisco and told her he had bought—if she liked it—a house on a site called Black Point, just opposite Alcatraz Island.

Like it! thought Jessie, when he took her there. She adored it!

The tract, of twelve acres, was at the very tip of Black Point, with an entrancing view of the Golden Gate. She walked among the flowers to the edge of the bluff, with the Pacific breeze lifting her hair. This, she thought, would be their ideal home. Although its title was clouded, that didn't trouble her—not yet—because so many land titles in early California were confused.

Black Point, Jessie's beloved home by the Golden Gate. The Frémont house was the one farthest out, at the end of the point. (An early, unsigned painting, now at Fort Mason. Courtesy of the Bancroft Library.)

However, this piece had been formally reserved by the government for military use, and Frémont had bought it from a man who might technically be called a squatter.

Jessie lived there happily for more than a year. "I loved this sea home so much that I had joy even in the tolling of the fogbell," she said.

The city schools were across the sand dunes, too far for the boys to go, so she taught them at home—but she was used to that. By now San Francisco was a city of one hundred thousand, with forty-six buildings of four stories and three of five stories. A good road connected Black Point with the city, so it was easy for Jessie to attend opera and concerts, and to find book-loving friends.

Still kind-hearted, she loved to give help. One protégé was Starr King, who became a famous preacher. Still another was the poet Bret Harte, then a struggling unknown. Jessie read his work, gave him advice, served him dinner every Sunday, and invited him to her literary "afternoons" to meet influential people. She also got him a government post that let him support himself and still have time for writing. In thanking her, he wrote,

"If I were cast upon a desert island, I should expect a savage to come forward with a three-cornered note from you to tell me that at your request I had been appointed Governor of the island at a salary of twenty-four hundred dollars."

But the idyll couldn't last, for trouble between the northern and southern states was deepening. One day a visiting senator told Frémont that President-elect Lincoln was considering him for Secretary of War, or as Minister to France.

"What do you wish?" Mr. Frémont asked Jessie.

"To stay here," she replied, "where I have taken root along with my rose bushes; otherwise, to do what you think best."

Frémont told the senator he didn't want an appointment then, but that if war came, he would serve wherever he was needed.

Although the mines were still rich, the mills and equipment were so expensive that by now Frémont was two million dollars in debt, with interest at twenty-four percent. Therefore, he decided to go to Europe to raise capital. Jessie planned to go with him, but one morning when she and Lily were riding down steep Russian Hill in a carriage, the horses bolted, the carriage rocked over cobblestones, its tongue broke, and both were thrown out. Although Lily was unhurt, Jessie's arm and leg were so badly injured that she had to give up the trip. Mr. Frémont went alone.

During his absence, the conflict between the states came to a head. The South was chiefly agricultural, while the North depended on industry and finance. They had been quarreling for years, partly because business men in the North and farmers in the South needed different kinds of laws, partly because they disagreed about slavery. Recently the quarrels were growing more bitter, with each side determined to extend its own system into the new lands of the West. When the Republicans—and Abraham Lincoln—won the election

Jessie in 1861, at the beginning of the Civil War. (From Jessie Benton Frémont, *by Catherine C. Phillips, 1935.)*

of 1860 on a strong pro-business platform, seven southern states seceded from the union and began to form a separate nation. This, said Lincoln, wouldn't be allowed. So the South decided to fight. On April 13, 1861, Southern troops bombarded Fort Sumter.

When this tragic word came over the new telegraph, Jessie knew it was the beginning of the conflict
she dreaded. With a sinking heart she followed the news
as Lincoln proclaimed a blockade of the South, and the
Confederate States chose Richmond as their capital.
Nothing would be the same, ever again. Her world was
gone.

In early June she received a letter from Mr. Frémont, saying he had been made Major-General of the
Regular Army to command the Western Division with
headquarters at St. Louis. He asked her to join him.

Sadly, she rented her Black Point home and directed
the packing. Sadly, on June 21, she started east, her arm
and foot still in splints. She was accompanied by her
family and also by a trained nurse, because she could
use only one hand.

A minister friend, who saw her off on the steamer,
gave her a bouquet of English violets and a copy of
Emerson's *Essays*.

"Here," he said. "Smell, read, and rest."

Jessie was on her way to war.

War!

1861-1865

IT WAS A LONG TRIP and a weary one for Jessie, with her injured arm, but by July 25, she and Mr. Frémont were in St. Louis. There they found his Department in a muddle.

Missouri was a "border state." That is, although it was officially in the Union, its people were divided. A Confederate flag was flying from a Southern enlistment headquarters, right there in the city. Rebels were camping in the countryside, some had fought Union troops, and the state governor sympathized with the South.

In addition, the Northern Army wasn't ready for war. Volunteers were pouring in—without blankets, tents, uniforms or shoes to outfit them. No money had come for their pay. Some men left, while others were near mutiny.

Overwhelmed, Mr. Frémont began to work fifteen or eighteen hours a day, and Jessie tried to help by copying confidential letters and carrying dispatches for officers to sign when they were ill.

One of her jobs was almost unbearable—writing notices to families of soldiers who had been killed. Once she said, "I wrote six letters today to break the hearts of mothers. It has thrown me into a panic."

Major General Frémont, in the Civil War. An early lithograph. (Courtesy of the Bancroft Library.)

MAJOR GEN! FREMONT.

The Sanitary Commission, forerunner of the Red Cross, has set up a treatment station near a battlefield. Throughout the Civil War Jessie worked for the Sanitary Commission. (From Frank Leslie's Illustrated Newspaper, *April, 1864.)*

She also found a project of her own—serving on the Sanitary Commission, forerunner of the Red Cross.

When she first visited the military hospital, she was horrified to see wounded soldiers lying in full sun from unshaded windows. She spent her own money for blue blinds to shut out the glare, and she called on hostile shopkeepers to plead for supplies.

These were often given because of her family. One man said, "This is not sent to the wife of the Yankee general, but to the daughter of Mrs. Benton who always gave to those who needed help."

Soon she received a visit from the famous Dorothea Dix, now Superintendent of Women Nurses for the Northern Armies. Miss Dix and Jessie found that overworked hospital orderlies didn't have time to feed their patients. Instead, they laid thick slices of bread, tin cups of coffee and hunks of salt pork on the chests of wounded men who were too sick to touch them. Appalled, Jessie and Miss Dix then began a campaign to secure volunteer aides for the wards, and they organized "circles" of women to make bandages and knit sweaters.

Lily tried to knit, but it was too much for her clumsy fingers. She toiled at it grimly until she achieved two dozen pairs of socks, no two of which were the same size or length. When she turned them in, with a mixture of pride and chagrin, the matron wryly said, "They'll have to go to men who have lost one leg."

In the East, that summer of 1861 was a disaster, with the Union armies in flight after the first Battle of Bull Run. It was no better in Missouri, where forty

*An attack on the St. Louis Police Court in June, 1861.
Frémont had just taken command in Missouri, and
violence was frequent. (By William Streeter. Courtesy
of the Missouri Historical Society. Negative #-Public
Buildings 460.)*

thousand rebels were seizing horses, food and clothing
from loyal citizens, burning bridges, wrecking trains
and attacking exposed units.

At last Frémont decided he must quiet the turmoil by
taking strong action. On August 30, just a month after

his arrival, he issued a proclamation which would place Missouri under martial law, shoot active rebels, confiscate their property, and set their slaves free. It was limited, for it merely freed the slaves of insurgents in this one area, but it was the first emancipation proclamation in the nation.

When the telegraph clicked out this astonishing news, it set off a national furor. Up to then the official reason for war had been to preserve the Union, but now the issue of slavery was out in the open. Some hailed Frémont as a crusader, while others thought he was courting disaster. His named was blazoned in headlines, and was on everyone's tongue.

However, within a few days a special messenger brought a letter from President Lincoln. "Should you shoot a man," he wrote, "the Confederates would very certainly shoot our best men in their hands in retaliation." He felt that freeing slaves would alarm the wavering Southern states that had not seceded, and he asked General Frémont to water down his proclamation, as if of his own free will.

Lincoln hadn't reckoned on the pride and determination of Jessie's husband. Once Mr. Frémont had defied a general and landed in a court martial. Now he said, "If I were to retract of my own accord, it would imply that I myself thought it wrong."

He wrote a letter for Jessie to copy, insisting that Lincoln send him an outright order, not a request, and he asked Jessie to deliver it in person. She willingly agreed.

Although she was still almost helpless from her injured arm, she sat up for two nights on a crowded train, living on tea and biscuits. By the time she reached Willard's Hotel in Washington, she was exhausted, rumpled, and looking forward to a bath and a night's rest. But she promptly sent Lincoln a note asking when she might bring him the letter.

To her surprise, the messenger returned almost at once with a card on which was written,

> *A. Lincoln.*
> *Now.*

Delaying the President would be an unthinkable rudeness, so Jessie hastily smoothed her dress and went to the White House, where Lincoln soon came to her, weary and sad.

"Well—" he said, and paused, apparently forgetting to offer her a seat. He was just as tall and awkward as she remembered, and even more stooped, and he had grown a beard.

When she handed him Frémont's letter, he carefully read it, moving to the chandelier for better light, while Jessie found herself a chair. At last the President sat down near her. "I have written to the general; he knows what I want done," he said.

She then told him why the proclamation was

needed in Missouri, but her words were useless. Even though Lincoln detested slavery, his purpose at that time was to preserve the Union, and he was determined not to make any move that would cause more states to secede.

"The general ought not to have done it; he should never have dragged the Negro into the war," he said. "It is a war for a great national object and the Negro has nothing to do with it."

Nothing to do with it! thought Jessie, for to her slavery was the greatest issue of all. However, she kept calm and only asked when she could have an answer.

"Maybe by tomorrow," said the President. "I have a great deal to do—tomorrow, if possible, or the next day."

"I will come for it," Jessie offered.

"No, I will send it to you, tomorrow or the day after." With a brief nod, President Lincoln was gone.

The next morning Jessie was called on by an old friend, Senator Francis Blair. "Well," he blustered, "who would have expected you to do such a thing as this, to come here and find fault with the president."

At first Jessie thought he was joking, but he was really angry.

"Look what you have done," he continued. "Made the president an enemy." He stayed with her for an hour, scolding her as if she were a child.

Jessie's heart sank, for she was sure Senator Blair knew exactly how the president felt. Instead of helping, she had made things worse.

After the Senator left, the hours seemed endless until Lincoln's reply came, formal and cold, saying that the proclamation would be declared void. Jessie's trip had been in vain. Wearily she returned to St. Louis and again took up the work of war.

During the next weeks waves of criticism mounted against Frémont. His Western Department was called corrupt and extravagant, and his army unit of Hungarians, the Zagonyi Guard, was said to be un-American. By October 24, after only one hundred days in Missouri, he was removed from his command.

Jessie considered this unfair, an outrage, and she was miserable. To her minister friend she wrote that she felt "struck down into the torment of outer darkness."

She wasn't the only indignant one, for Frémont's dismissal set off a national outcry. Flags flew at half mast, bands and crowds waited to meet him. Most newspapers supported him, saying that Lincoln's action was a "heavy calamity," and that it caused a "funeral gloom." A commission finally investigated the Western Department, finding blunders but no corruption. Although Frémont had not shown great skill as a general, he had freed Missouri from guerrilla bands and had made its important river ports secure. His reputation for personal honesty came through undamaged.

Jessie was also called blameless. Dorothea Dix declared, "The name Jessie Frémont is held in love and reverence everywhere in the West."

Jessie and her family now returned East, where, a few months later, they were "surprised and shocked" to be invited to a ball at the White House. Many objected to dancing and feasting in wartime, and Jessie, sorrowing for relatives who had been killed on the rebel side, didn't want to attend. However, when Lincoln sent word that he especially wished to see General Frémont, she agreed to go.

It was a tragic event, for the president's son, Willie, not quite twelve years old, had ridden his pony in a cold rain and was seriously ill with a fever. Although Lincoln tried to cancel the ball, it was too late, so he eliminated the dancing, but received his guests in the elaborately decorated East Room. In speaking to Jessie and her husband, he said his son was very ill, and that he feared for the result. As she described it:

The Marine Band at the foot of the steps
filled the house with music while the boy lay
dying above. A sadder face than that of the
president I have rarely seen.

A few days later Willie's funeral procession left from the same room, with the potted palms still in place. "It is hard, hard, hard, to have him die," the grieving father said.

The rest of 1862 the war continued to be bloody, with neither side able to win. Slaves were fleeing to the

Ball at the White House. When Jessie attended this ball, she was shocked, because Willie Lincoln was upstairs, dying. (From Leslie's Illustrated Newspaper, *February, 1862.)*

Union armies, and some were being formed into black battalions that fought bravely.

In Washington, the president began to think he must change course, because people in the North were more and more determined to end slavery. Moreover, there was fear that Great Britain might give aid to the South—something that wouldn't happen if it became a war to free the slaves.

Therefore, in the fall, Lincoln announced that in any state that was still fighting by January 1, 1863, all slaves would be considered free, and on that day he formally issued the Emancipation Proclamation. When Jessie heard about it, she was overjoyed. Now at last, she thought, it was truly a righteous war. More than that, she felt it vindicated her Mr. Frémont. Everybody could now see that he had been right all along.

Soon afterward she discovered that the Zagonyi Guard, Hungarians who had served under Frémont in Missouri, were receiving no aid for crippled soldiers or for families of their dead. For a while Jessie supported some of them herself, but she soon decided that publicity would help them more. So she wrote to a publisher suggesting a book, and he offered to pay her a six hundred dollar advance when she turned in the manuscript.

With typical Jessie-enthusiasm, she now told her family, "I won't either eat nor sleep until *The Story of the Guard* is complete." She then shut herself in her bedroom and set to work on what she happily called her "bookling."

She did, of course, eat and sleep, but she cut even that to a minimum. Twelve days later the editor was astonished to have her walk into his office with manuscript in hand and ask for the promised advance. In October it was published—a lively account. In describing a camp pitched in a swamp, she wrote, "Water is a very large thing indeed; and not a pleasant bedfellow." She quoted a guardsman as saying of an elderly corporal named Wamba, "It is my private impression that Wamba is made of wood—head and all." Because it was one of the first books to tell hero stories about the Civil War, it sold extremely well and was even translated into German.

By 1864, the turning point of the war had been passed at Gettysburgh, but people were weary, and wanted it to end. With another election near, Lincoln was bitterly attacked as a blunderer.

"We went in for a rail-splitter and we have got one," was frequently said.

However, he was too strong to be defeated for the Republican nomination, so Mr. Frémont was asked to be the candidate for a third, anti-Lincoln party. He consented, and was nominated.

This, Jessie thought, was a dreadful mistake, for if the Republicans were divided, the Democrats would surely win. Some of Frémont's friends added their voices to hers, advising him not to run. Urged by friends, urged by Jessie, he withdrew—thus writing a page of history. If he had run, he would have split the Republican vote, and Lincoln would almost certainly have lost.

Many people objected to the Civil War and thought the North should work out a just peace with the South. This is a bitter protest against the tragedy of war. (From Harper's Weekly, *September 2, 1864.)*

Jessie and Mr. Frémont were both well content. When other friends protested, he said, "My only consideration was the welfare of the Republican party," and she calmly added, "The general and I think alike in this matter."

She would be happy to return to private life.

SIXTEEN

Shadows on the Walls

1865-1873

WHILE THE CIVIL WAR RAGED, sorrow had come to Jessie, for her dearest sister Eliza had died, aged only forty-one, and this was a heartbreak. Not only Eliza was gone. Many of the merry young Virginia cousins had laid down their lives for the Confederacy. The South was shattered, cities in ruins, farms and fields laid waste. Cherry Grove was part of Jessie's past now, a past she could never regain.

She would have liked to return to San Francisco, to Black Point, but that was impossible because the army had claimed it under the old proclamation that reserved it for military use. Although some of its landowners were paid, the Frémont place was simply confiscated. The house, garden, laurel thickets, and even the summit of the bluff were leveled for earthworks. So Jessie couldn't go back after all to her beloved cottage by the Golden Gate, with its sunshine and fog, its breakers and winds.

A passenger boat on the Hudson River, at the time Jessie was living at Pocaho. She must have often traveled on boats like this. (From Harper's Weekly. *Courtesy of the Metropolitan Museum of Art, New York City.)*

She remained in New York City, helping with hospitals, while Lincoln was reelected and the Civil War ran its course. She was in New York when the President was assassinated. From there she observed the first groping steps to reunite the nation.

But she wanted a home, as much as possible like Black Point where she had been so happy. Finally, after a long search, she found a hundred-acre estate with a large stone house, two miles north of Tarrytown, and overlooking the broad reach of the Hudson River called

the Tappan Zee. Mountains towered in the blue dis
tance, while nearby flowering paths led through dee
woods. Jessie kept its Indian name, "Pocaho," and calle
it "a blur of beauty."

Furnishing Pocaho was pure joy. During the w
Mr. Frémont had sold his mines for more than six m
lion dollars, and even after paying his debts he was st
wealthy, so Jessie had plenty of money to work wi
She had the library carpeted in moss green, with bo
to the ceiling, and a three-step ladder for reaching
topmost shelves.

It was a busy, happy home. When Mr. Frém
was away on business, as often happened, Jessie m
go to New York to attend dinners, plays or concerts,
when he was there, they lived quietly, taking a
walk almost every evening. The young people
quently sat on the floor by the fireplace, munc
cakes and apples while Jessie read to them or told
ries about her adventurous life. Although she was
forty-one, her hair was turning so white that fr
called it "startling." It was still wavy, and she
wore her favorite violet color. Mr. Frémont once
tionately said, "She contents the eye."

She loved her children enough to let them d
in their own ways. Lily was twenty-three, frank,
what blunt, passionately fond of horses and ridir
the back of one of Lily's portraits Jessie wrote.
cious, unshakable as Bunker Hill." Charley wa
teen, a slim, dark-eyed, restless boy who wante
a sailor. And Frank was eleven—dreamy, studiou

pianist who often played in the night. In one letter Jessie called the differences among her children "an unending source of wonder," and said she wanted them free to follow their own desires.

"Lil shall make her own bridle paths," she wrote. "Charley shall drink up Tappan Zee. Frank shall play his piano when he likes, if I have to put it in a tree house." This last was an answer to those who criticized his nighttime music.

They had an almost continuous stream of visitors— relatives, writers, scientists, politicians. One was the painter Bierstadt, whose picture of the Golden Gate at sunset hung above Jessie's library mantel. "If I should never enter that gate again," she exclaimed when she saw it for the first time, "this will keep me from grieving too much. I must never part with it."

Another famous guest was the portrait-painter Fagnani, who came with his wife. He had just finished painting the "nine most beautiful women in New York," and now, after painting Jessie, he declared she was the tenth.

In 1868, Jessie had the joy of unveiling a statue of her father in Lafayette Park in St. Louis. More than forty thousand people were there, including hundreds of school children dressed in white and carrying red roses, Benton's favorite flower. While the band played, Jessie drew the cord and the white drapery parted to show a statue of heroic size, facing westward. Its bronze glinted in the sun, the children threw their roses at its base, and at that moment the train to San Francisco,

Lily, Jessie's daughter and lifetime companion.
(Courtesy of the Bancroft Library.)

passing on a nearby track, paused and saluted with whistle and flags.

Jessie was as tender-hearted as ever. Hearing about famine in the South, she wrote to senators and representatives, and got a relief ship and an order for supplies. She secured back pay and positions for more than thirty union officers, pleading for them so eloquently that Judge Black of Pennsylvania told her, "Your geese are all swans."

No one knows how much money she gave away, or how many people she befriended, for she never discussed them, but one surviving list names eight young men and twelve young women who received, in one year, anonymous gifts of tuition to various colleges.

Meanwhile, Mr. Frémont had a brand new project —founding the Memphis and El Paso railroad, to run from Virginia to Southern California. He secured land grants in Texas, bought property in California, got franchises in Arizona and Arkansas.

All this required so much money that he went to Europe to raise it, taking Jessie and the children. Being celebrities, they had an audience with the Queen of Denmark and attended the wedding ball for Denmark's crown prince. Best of all, they visited Jessie's youngest sister Susan, who was still married and living in France.

However, as always with Mr. Frémont, the good times didn't last. In 1873, eight years after buying Pocaho, his railroad collapsed, and he was blamed because his agents had falsely declared, without his knowledge, that the bonds he sold in France were backed by the

Jessie in Pocaho days. (From Memoirs of My Life, *by John Charles Frémont, 1887.)*

United States Government. Debts of the enterprise were so deep and lawsuits so expensive, that the Frémont fortune was wiped out, and Jessie felt a "dizzying drop" from wealth into poverty.

She wrote to a friend, "It is an inextricable mass out of which I can glean only an impression of millions of dollars of railroad bonds floated abroad which brought profit only to the agent, advertisements published abroad that misrepresented the whole railroad picture, of which Mr. Frémont knew nothing."

As long as she could she clung to Pocaho, cutting down on servants and charities and trips to Washington. Nothing she could do was enough. Even though an investigation cleared her husband of any wrong-doing, they had to sell not only the estate, but also the books, paintings, furniture—even the treasured picture of Golden Gate. Instead of living in a luxurious mansion, she had to move to a "musty, ill-lighted house in town."

Two children were still with them: Frank, the pianist, who had gone to West Point briefly, but returned home because he developed tuberculosis; Lily, still unmarried, still Jessie's close companion. Only Charley was away, having just graduated as an ensign from the Naval College at Annapolis.

Dry-eyed, Jessie went through the ordeal of the sale, salvaging what she could, and showing so much strength that a friend called her "gallant Jessie."

She herself commented, "I am like a deeply built ship; I drive best under a strong wind."

One morning while she was showing a stranger through the house, he commented on its size and good taste. With a sigh she gazed fondly at her beautiful home, which she must leave.

"The rooms are large," she agreed. "They have

held much happiness. The new owners will find few shadows on the walls."

Even so, she was looking ahead, not back. As yet she hadn't told anyone, not even her Mr. Frémont, but she had a plan for earning an income of her own.

Dauntless Jessie

1873-1902

SOON JESSIE was settled in an "ugly but comfortable" house at Seventy-seventh Street and Madison Avenue, in New York City, and it was time to put her grand plan into effect. Dressed in her best, she called on Robert Bonner, editor of the *New York Ledger*, to suggest a series of articles about her exciting life. Mr. Bonner, who offered to pay one hundred dollars each, thought it would take her months, but she worked day and night and brought them to him in just sixteen days. *Harper's* (a literary magazine) and *Wide Awake* (a magazine for children) also promised to buy as much as she could produce, so she spent long hours at her desk.

One letter to a friend said, "I am very pleased with myself, for I have four columns all finished—four hundred dollars this week already, and now it runs easily."

It was exciting but bittersweet to live through the old days—Washington—St. Louis—Cherry Grove—the

Isthmus of Panama—Bear Valley. She wrote vividly, bringing each scene alive, and called it "a memory game where the cards get an occasional blob of tears as I play it here—alone."

But she soon had more to do than write, because Mr. Frémont accepted an appointment as Governor of the Territory of Arizona. It was a new, raw country, he

Jessie in a portrait painted in 1880, about the time she moved to California. (From Jessie Benton Frémont, *by Catherine C. Phillips, 1935.)*

said, and the journey would be long and hard. Nevertheless, she eagerly set out, along with Lily, Frank, who was still not well, and Frank's big dog, Thor.

The first part was easy—by train to San Francisco, with cheering crowds at many stops along the way. They were offered banquets at Omaha and Chicago, which they refused, and in San Francisco, which they accepted.

From there they went by train to Yuma, Arizona, and then started an eight-day journey through the tawny yellow desert, their transportation being an army ambulance with a blue body and canvas sides, drawn by six large mules.

"I pity you—I pity you," said General William Sherman, who was returning from an inspection trip there. "Going over that road, there are places where I held my breath and shut my eyes. You will cry and say your prayers."

They spent eight days in the desert, sleeping out at night. The driver took extreme care on the flinty path, "but weren't we bruised!" Jessie exclaimed. Each day was a long ordeal of pitiless heat, to somehow live through. Thor was miserable, too. He got cactus thorns in his feet, tried to pull them out with his teeth, and then they pierced his tongue. Lily was up most of one night, patiently removing them one by one.

After passing the bleak desert they climbed steeply through shady pine forests to the town of Prescott, more than a mile high. Since this was the site of an army barracks, Jessie found a good, though small, social life here, with officers and their wives, a dramatic club, theater, brick school house, and a post band.

"Imagine all this up here!" she wrote to a friend. She loved the glorious sunsets, and the desert flowers after a rain.

Soon she was as busy as ever, making friends and entertaining often with the aid of a Chinese cook named Ah Chung. Everything was strange. Even Thor had new problems. "He can't dig in this hard earth, so we bury his bones for him. He is greatly pleased," Jessie commented.

When she learned that there was no hospital, she wrote to the sisters of St. Joseph in St. Louis, with the result that two nuns came riding up the trail. The day they arrived was blistering hot, and when Jessie saw their heavy black habits, she was appalled.

"You can never wear such clothes in this climate," she protested.

"What can be done?" they mildly asked.

"I don't know. But we shall see." She sat down at her desk and dashed off a letter, and soon the nuns, with their superior's approval, were wearing cooler clothing.

As always, Jessie reached out to offer help. She tried to encourage the Mojave women to make their traditional pottery. She also visited the local school and was asked to make a talk. Her story about Marie Antoinette aroused so much interest that from then on she spoke at the school every Friday. She said she was "trying to put flesh and garments on the skeletons of their thin outline history course."

"You're a blessed lunatic," one woman said, when she heard about the weekly talks.

Lunacy? thought Jessie. If so, it was lunacy twice blessed, for it eased her homesickness to give so much pleasure.

In the dry climate of Prescott, Frank recovered and Jessie's fragile lungs were well, but the altitude affected her heart. She felt weak and listless, with occasional attacks of dizziness. One day Lily and Mr. Frémont found her lying on the floor in a stupor, and when they called the post physician, he said she must permanently leave. So she made a lonely journey back to New York, where more and still more articles poured from her flying pen.

In 1883, after five years as governor, Mr. Frémont resigned, to Jessie's supreme happiness, for now she thought they could be together for always and always. Although he was past seventy, he still seemed young because of his close-cropped hair, slender figure, and elastic step. Returning East, he lived with her in New York.

One day after they had attended church, an item in a newspaper called them "a venerable couple who in their day were better known than any pair since George Washington and his wife. The man sat straight as a ramrod and wearing a derby hat and dark suit with natty fitting boots." The item mentioned the silver sheen of Jessie's exquisite hair, and her perfect repose, and concluded, "They are the handsomest old couple in the city."

Since they still hadn't been paid for Black Point,

*John Charles Frémont and Jessie, standing close
together, and their daughter Lily, at the side. This
picture was taken while they were on an excursion to
see the redwoods of California. (Courtesy of the
Bancroft Library.)*

Mr. Frémont made countless attempts to collect, and
they were both busy writing. In 1887, each published
a book: the first volume of his *Memoirs of My Life*,
written with Jessie's help, and her *Souvenirs of My
Time*, which was a collection of her magazine pieces.

But when he fell seriously ill with bronchitis, the
doctor said he needed a warmer climate. This would
mean an expensive move, for which they hadn't enough
money, so Jessie boldly sought help from Collis P. Hunt-

ington, a railroad magnate. When she told her story, Mr. Huntington offered to pay for the journey.

She had reckoned without her Mr. Frémont, who flatly refused to accept charity. Thin and pale, he stared out of the window, not speaking, not touching the chicken broth she had especially made.

Jessie was miserable. "Here we were, lovers for forty-seven years, having our first lovers' quarrel!" she said.

A day later Mr. Huntington came to call, with railroad tickets and a check for expenses. "Our railroad goes over your buried campfires and climbs a grade you jogged over on a mule. I rather think we owe you this," he said, and under his urging the invalid at last agreed to go.

He and Jessie and Lily then moved to Los Angeles, where they lived in a small rented house on Oak Street, still writing, still making friends. They were proud of their sons, who were both in the armed services, Charley a commander in the United States Navy, and Frank a captain in the Army. They were both big fellows, tall, sturdy, black-haired and black-eyed, and bearded.

By 1889, Mr. Frémont was seventy-six years old, and Jessie was sixty-five. Still urging the Black Point claim, he paid a very long visit to Washington, D.C., where he lived in Charley's home. His pleas bore some fruit, for the next spring he was reinstated as Major-General Retired of the United States Army, with a pension of six thousand dollars a year. This would mean an end to poverty, and he sent Jessie a jubilant telegram.

However, only two months later, still in the East, he again fell ill of a ruptured appendix, or perhaps an ulcer. That day Jessie received a telegram from Charley saying, "Father is ill." And a few hours later another message brought her world crashing down. "Father is dead." It was July 13, 1890.

Jessie's sons. At left is Commander John Charles Frémont, United States Navy; at right is Captain Frank Preston Frémont, United States Army. (From Jessie Benton Frémont, *by Catherine C. Phillips, 1935.)*

At first she was numb—"like a paralysis"—for Mr. Frémont had been the center of her life since she was seventeen years old. With difficulty she roused herself enough to wire Charley a request that her last telegram should be buried with her husband, along with the miniature of her which he still carried wherever he went, the one Kit Carson had taken to him across the plains.

This was done. "Your message and your picture I put into his hand," Charley wrote to her. "I folded up the telegram and wrapped it and the miniature in the ribbons which were tied to it."

Jessie's husband was then buried without her presence at Trinity Church in New York City.

Grieving as she was, Jessie found relief in action. First she tried to clear Mr. Frémont's name from the cloud of the court-martial, and from the falsely advertised railroad. She wrote letters, conducted interviews, and published articles and documents. Then, having done everything she could, she turned to her own affairs, for even though she would always miss him, she still loved life.

Her remaining years were happy. The women of Los Angeles raised money and built her a cottage at the corner of Hoover and Twenty-eighth Streets. Calling it her "retreat," she lived here with Lily in genteel poverty, her chief income being a tiny widow's pension of $2,000 a year. The famous flocked to her door. A young sculptor, Gutzon Borglum, who would later carve out giant figures of presidents in the Black Hills, came to make a bust of her. Newspaper editors visited her, along with politicians, teachers, writers. She especially liked the young people of the neighborhood, who often sat at her feet while she told them stories.

One chief delight was her large correspondence. "I wait for the postman as a child does for Santa Claus," she once said.

"The Retreat," Jessie's home in Los Angeles, which was given to her by the women of that city. (From Jessie Benton Frémont, *by Catherine C. Phillips, 1935.)*

Just at the close of the century, when she was seventy-six, she had a serious fall, which injured her hip and forced her to use a detested wheel chair. Even there she continued to write and to receive visitors. One was President William McKinley, who bowed over her hand and gave her the gardenia from his buttonhole.

On Christmas Eve, 1902, many packages and letters arrived, and in delight Jessie said to Lily, "Let me have my Christmas tonight! Somehow this year I can't wait."

Agreeing, Lily helped her open gifts and messages.

When they were through, Jessie said, "I am very happy over such attention, but I am tired. Now I will sleep."

These were her last words, for she didn't awaken. Two days later she drew a shorter breath—and stopped.

As she had wished, there was only a simple service, followed by cremation and the shipment of her ashes to New York. Today Jessie and Mr. Frémont lie side by side at Piermont-on-the-Hudson, just across the river from their beloved Pocaho.

Jessie's life, which she had lived almost entirely for others, was over. But her influence was not, even though there is no way to measure it. No record exists of the young people she assisted through scholarships, nor can anyone say how much aid she gave to the Zagonyi Guard, or to veterans of the Civil War, or to the Indians of California, or those of Arizona.

By helping her husband write his reports she made them more readable—and who can say what effect that

The last picture of Jessie, taken after the fall that confined her to a wheel chair. (From Jessie Benton Frémont, *by Catherine C. Phillips, 1935.)*

had on settling the West? By fighting slavery she helped keep California a free state—and who knows what effect that had on the Civil War? We can only guess what might have happened if she had urged Mr. Frémont to run for president in 1864—splitting the Republican vote and resulting in Lincoln's defeat. She was one of America's great popular heroines, for she and her husband were idolized in their day much as Charles and Anne Lindbergh were idolized a century later.

Although the women's rights movement didn't begin until she was well launched into her own exciting life, Jessie considered women capable and wanted them to be recognized. One day a friend, in commenting on a bright young acquaintance, said she had a man's mind.

"By that I suppose you mean to make her a supreme compliment," Jessie retorted. "A *good mind*! If so, let us say it so. You can safely accord woman a fair share of brains."

She herself had more than a fair share, which she used to the full. Twin threads were woven through her life: excitement, and love. She had zest for whatever came and was always willing to do whatever she must. She had love for her husband, for her father, for her family and friends, for suffering humanity, for life. She was a spendthrift of time and emotion, with a gift for joy. When things were going well, she accepted them with grace; when she met defeat, she rejected despair.

"I drive best under a strong wind," she once said.

For Jessie, the wind was always strong.

BIBLIOGRAPHY

Primary Sources

BOOKS

Benton, Thomas Hart. *Thirty Years' View.* New York, 1854.

Bigelow, John. *Life and Public Service of John Charles Frémont.* New York, 1856.

Buck, Franklin A. *A Yankee Trader in the Gold Rush.* Boston and New York, 1930.

Carvalho, S. N. *Incidents of Travel and Adventure in the Far West with Frémont's Last Expedition.* New York, 1856.

Colton, Walter. *Three Years in California.* New York and Cincinnati, 1852.

Ellett, Elizabeth Fries. *Queens of American Society, a Memoir of Mrs. Frémont.* New York, 1867.

Encyclopoedia Brittanica, Inc. William Benton, Publisher. *The Annals of America.* Chicago, London, 1968.

Frémont, Elizabeth Benton. *Recollections of Elizabeth Benton Frémont, Daughter of the Pathfinder General John C. Frémont and Jessie Benton Frémont His Wife.* New York, 1912.

Frémont, Jessie Benton. *Far West Sketches.* Boston, 1890.

Frémont, Jessie Benton. *Mother Lode Narratives.* Edited by Shirley Sargent. Ashland, Oregon, 1970.

Frémont, Jessie Benton. *Souvenirs of My Time*. Boston, 1887.

Frémont, Jessie Benton. *Story of the Guard, a Chronicle of the War*. Cambridge, Massachusetts, 1862.

Frémont, Jessie Benton. *The Will and the Way Stories*. Boston, 1891.

Frémont, Jessie Benton. *A Year of American Travel*. New York, 1878.

Frémont, John Charles. *Memoirs of My Life, a Retrospect of Fifty Years*. New York, 1887.

Frémont, John Charles. *The Exploring Expedition to the Rocky Mountains, Oregon and California*. (Third Expedition.) New York, 1849.

Frémont, John Charles. *A Report on an Exploration of the Country Lying Between the Missouri River and the Rocky Mountains on the Line of the Kansas and Great Platte Rivers*. (First Expedition.) Senate Document No. 243, 27th Congress, 3rd Session, 1843.

Frémont, John Charles. *A Report of the Exploring Expedition to Oregon and North California in the Years 1843–44*. (Second Expedition.) Washington, 1845.

Hawley, H. H., Publisher. *Songs for Free Men. A Collection of Words and Campaign and Popular Songs for the People, Adapted to Familiar and Popular Melodies and Designed to Promote the Course of "Free Speech, Free Press, Free Soil, Free Men, and Frémont."* Utica, New York, 1856.

Johnson, T. T. *Sights in the Gold Region*. New York, 1850.

Marryat, Frank. *Mountains and Molehills*. New York, 1855.

Polk, James K. *The Diary of President James K. Polk During His Presidency*. Ed. by Milo Milton Quaife. 4 vols. Chicago, 1910.

Revere, J. W. *A Tour of Duty in California*. New York and Boston, 1849.

Schmucker, Samuel M. (Also spelled Smucker.) *The Life and Love of J. C. Frémont*. New York, 1856.

Taylor, Bayard. *El Dorado*. 1850. New York and London, 1864.

Upham, C. W. *Life, Explorations and Public Services of John Charles Frémont*. Boston, 1856.

Woodworth. *The Young American's Life of Frémont*. New York, 1856.

MANUSCRIPTS *(In Bancroft Library)*

Frémont and the Campaign of 1856. (Collection of pamphlets, etc.)

Frémont, Elizabeth Benton. *Memoirs and notes.*

Frémont, Elizabeth Benton. *Scrapbook.*

Frémont, Jessie Benton. *Letters to Elizabeth.*

Frémont, Jessie Benton. *Letters Written by Jessie Benton Frémont, 1862–1897.*

Frémont, Jessie Benton. *Memoirs of Jessie Benton Frémont.*

Frémont, Jessie Benton. Scrapbook of Clippings.

Frémont, John Charles. *Great Events During the Life of Major General John C. Frémont.* (This is volume II of his Memoirs.)

Martin, Thomas S. *Narrative of John C. Frémont's Expedition in California in 1845–46 and Subsequent Events in California Down to 1853.*

Secondary Sources

BOOKS

Bartlett, Ruhl Jacobs. *John C. Frémont and the Republican Party*. Columbus, Ohio, 1930.

Dellenbaugh, Frederick S. *Frémont and '49.* New York, 1914.

De Voto, Bernard. *Across the Wide Missouri.* New York, 1947.

De Voto, Bernard. *The Year of Decision 1846.* Boston, 1943.

Egan, Ferol. *Frémont: Explorer for a Restless Nation.* New York, 1977.

Holliday, J. S. *The World Rushed In.* New York, 1981.

Jackson, Joseph Henry. *Gold Rush Album.* New York, 1949.

McCullough, David. *The Path Between the Seas: The Creation of the Panama Canal, 1870–1914.* New York, 1977.

Nevins, Allan. *Frémont: Pathmarker of the West.* New York, 1939.

Nevins, Allan. *Frémont, the West's Greatest Adventurer.* New York and London, 1928.

Palmer, John Williamson. *Pioneer Days in California.* Olympic Valley, California, 1977.

Phillips, Catherine Coffin. *Jessie Benton Frémont: A Woman Who Made History.* San Francisco, 1935.

Rather, Lois. *Jessie Frémont at Black Point.* Oakland, California, 1974.

Sandburg, Carl. *Abraham Lincoln: The Prairie Years and The War Years.* New York, 1954.

Sunset Books and Sunset Magazine, editors. *Gold Rush Country.* Menlo Park, California, 1957.

Scherer, James A. B., *The First Forty-Niner.* New York, 1925.

I N D E X